THE HIDDEN MATHEMATICS OF THE QURAN

REVEALING THE NUMBERS, PATTERNS, AND THE MYSTERY OF 19 IN THE QURAN

Faiyaz Abbas

QCS
PUBLICATIONS

QCS PUBLICATIONS
Mumbai, India

First Edition, 2026

ISBN: 978-93-5759-696-1

This book reflects the author's research, interpretations, and perspectives. While every effort has been made to ensure accuracy and clarity, the content is presented for academic, educational, and contemplative purposes only. The views expressed herein are those of the author and do not claim to represent any institution, organization, or authority. Readers are encouraged to engage with the material thoughtfully and independently. Neither the author nor the publisher assumes liability for any loss or damage arising from the use or interpretation of the information contained in this book.

بسم الله الرحمن الرحيم

In The Name of God – The Gracious, The Merciful

عَلَيْهَا تِسْعَةَ عَشَرَ ۝

"Over it are Nineteen" (74: 30)

There is enough light for those who wish to see.

- Imam Ali Ibn Abi Talib

DEDICATION

This book is dedicated to my parents, brothers, wife, daughter, and son for their unwavering support and inspiration. This work would not have been possible without their constant encouragement and understanding. This exploration was possible due to my extensive conversations and frequent interactions with my uncles.

NOTE TO THE READER

This work is a **significantly revised and expanded version** of my earlier publication, *Cracking the Divine Code*. It has been retitled to better reflect its depth, scope, and clarity.

In this book, you will find **additional examples**, **clearer explanations**, and **expanded tables** that further illuminate the subject. The structure has been refined to provide a smoother reading experience, while preserving the essence of the original research. This edition includes minor refinements and supplementary material not present in earlier or alternate formats.

EPIGRAPH

This book is presented in a way that makes it easy for anyone to verify the astounding mathematical facts in the Quran. This book's primary goal is to help readers appreciate the magnificence of the Holy Quran - the book written in God's own words. Some of the work presented in this book is also an online collection of the contributions made by other Muslim brothers worldwide. A simple search in any electronic Quran file allows anyone to verify the counts of letters and words, and to check the links and connections of phrases and words by their chapter and verse numbers.

DISCLAIMER

TABLE OF CONTENTS

1

THE SEED OF DOUBT

Plunge into the depths until you reach the truth - Imam Ali

In the quiet depths of contemplation, a seed of doubt takes root in the hearts of believers. It is a doubt that has lingered for over 1400 years, casting a shadow of uncertainty over the compilation and preservation of the Quran.

The origins of this doubt trace back to the early days of Islam, to a time when the Prophet Muhammed (S) delivered his final sermon, leaving behind two weighty things: the book of God and his descendants. It is well known among Muslims that the Quran is the book of God, a divine revelation containing guidance for all of humanity. Yet, despite this clarity, questions persist about the completeness of the Quran as it exists today.

History tells us of a period following the death of Prophet Muhammed (S), during the caliphate of Umar ibn Khattab when the Quran was compiled into a single manuscript. This act, attributed to Umar ibn Khattab, raises doubts about the completeness of the compilation process. Was the Quran truly compiled in its entirety, or was it merely the best available compilation at the time?

The doubt deepens as we reflect on the Prophet's last words regarding "the Book of God" as one of the two weighty things he left behind. If the Quran was not fully compiled into a book during his lifetime, why did the Prophet emphasize the word "Book" of God instead of using the word "Quran"?

This doubt about the Quran is not confined to a specific sect or denomination within Islam. It cuts across Sunni and Shia divides, troubling the minds of scholars and believers alike. It is a doubt that raises eyebrows and silences debates, for it strikes at the very core of faith and belief.

On one side of the divide, there exists a belief in the concept of *"tahreef"* – the reduction or alteration of the Quran – as documented in history and accepted as a reality by many. On the other side stands the belief in the Quran as the complete and unaltered guidance from God, a miraculous revelation that transcends the bounds of human understanding.

In the face of these conflicting narratives, believers grapple with the question: Was the Quran truly well-guarded as God proclaimed in its verse (15:9): *"Indeed it is We who have sent down the Message; and it is We who will guard it"*, or did the hands of history tamper with its sacred words? And again, was the Quran compiled by God as proclaimed in its verse (75:17): *"Surely it is for Us to compile it..."*, or did historical personalities interfere with its sacred compilation?

To resolve this conflict, we must embark on a journey of exploration and discovery, confronting this seed of doubt face-to-face. For only through exploration and enlightenment can we hope to uncover the answers that have eluded us for centuries.

2

THE ROLE OF MATHEMATICS AS A GUIDE

With this seed of doubt, rooted in the hearts of believers, a call to exploration beckons us forward. Can we unravel the mysteries shrouding the compilation of the Quran and uncover the truth hidden within the placement of its verses and chapters?

The Language of God

To uncover the patterns and codes hidden within the text of the Quran, we need a precise and reliable instrument as a guide. One of the most indispensable tools for such research is Mathematics.

Scholars and philosophers have long asserted that *"Mathematics is the language in which God has written the universe."* This belief stems from the observation that the intricacies of the laws of physics, the elegance of geometric patterns, and the harmony of musical compositions all hint at a deep-rooted connection between mathematics and the underlying fabric of reality. Mathematics is so deeply intertwined with the Universe that the Greek philosopher Pythagoras once declared, *"All is Number"*.

If mathematics is the language of the creator, then this principle could apply not only to the physical world but also to the exploration of divine texts. The Creator, who brought into existence a world governed by mathematical laws, may have embedded similar principles within the Quran – a book written by God.

Could it be that the Quran was a complex puzzle waiting to be solved, and Mathematics is the key to unlocking its secrets? By applying mathematical analysis, can we uncover hidden layers of links and structure within the text that may not be immediately apparent? Can mathematical analysis reveal that the compilation of the Quran is not a product of chance, but rather a meticulously crafted masterpiece?

Imagine a journey where the power of mathematics serves as our guide, leading us through the intricate arrangements of verses and chapters within the Quran. Can we demonstrate, through mathematical principles, that the Quran is a work of unparalleled precision and complexity? Beyond its linguistic marvels, could the Quran also hold within its pages a mathematical miracle waiting to be discovered? Is there a distinct mathematical style of writing embedded within its text, one that defies replication and points to the opus of God?

Consider the Quranic verses that mention specific numbers, such as *"Over it are Nineteen" (74:30)* and *"the seven often-repeated verses" (15:87)*. Could these numerical references be more than mere mentions? Do they hint at a deeper connection between the Quran and mathematics, inviting us to explore their intertwined perfection?

Setting aside our doubts, we must prepare to embark on a journey of exploration with an open mind and a broad vision, to observe the possibilities that lie before us. For in the pursuit of truth, guided by mathematics, the universal language of the world, we may uncover a revelation beyond comprehension – a proof to the divine origins of the Quran and the intricate beauty of God's words in numbers.

3

THE VILLAINOUS SHADOW OF HISTORY

In our quest for truth, we face a hidden antagonist. We are confronted by the villainous shadow of history, which has set up a confusing maze of incorrectly recorded narratives and weak narrations introduced over time, casting doubt upon the completeness of the Quran. In its guise as the villain, history seeks to obscure the path of enlightenment with tales of incompleteness and alteration, known as *"tahreef"* in the Quran.

Many scholars, swayed by these weak narrations and historical traditions, argue that the Quran we possess today, though sufficient, is not complete. According to them, the original text revealed to Prophet Muhammed (S) was much more than what we possess today. The popular claim that the Quran is unchanged is simply not supported by history.

Throughout history, several narrations have hinted at the existence of verses or chapters that were once known among the early companions but did not make it into the final compilation of the Qur'an. A famous narration mentions that textual material was physically lost under unusual circumstances. There are also references in history to alternate arrangements and longer compilations of the Quran.

Although these historical narratives remain doubtful about their own authenticity and reliability, and often conflict with the words of the Quran, they wield a formidable influence, shaping the beliefs and perceptions of many scholars and believers alike.

Yet, amidst the shadowy recesses of history, there exists a steadfast belief in the complete preservation of the Quran – a belief upheld by scholars from the earliest periods of Islam to the present century. These scholars adamantly oppose any suggestion of distortion or incompleteness in the Quran, affirming its divine protection and integrity. These scholars agree that the Quran currently possessed by Muslims is exactly the same Quran that was revealed to the Holy Prophet, and it has not been altered.

The battleground is set, with history on one side, wielding its arsenal of weak narrations and dubious traditions, and the defenders of the Quran on the other, steadfast in their conviction of its complete preservation and divine compilation.

Can mathematics be our hero in this epic struggle against history's villainous grip? Can we harness the power of mathematics to combat the distortions of history and unveil the truth hidden within the Quran? Can we separate the wheat from the chaff by using the diversity of mathematics?

In the face of historical uncertainty and doubt, mathematics stands as a beacon of clarity and precision, offering a path forward through its undeniable logic and irrefutable truths. With mathematics as our guide and numbers as our light, we embark on a bold journey to confront the shadows of history and hope to emerge victorious in our quest for truth.

4

THE DUAL CHALLENGE

As we prepare to embark on our journey, we realize we are not merely facing a single battle. We stand at the crossroads, challenged on two fronts – by history on one hand, and by the Quran on the other. The challenge posed by history is about the Compilation and Completeness of the Quran, while the challenge posed by the Quran is about the Composition and the chef-d'oeuvre, the Masterwork of the Quran.

On one side of the arena, we confront the challenge posed by history, a challenge we seek to overcome with the assistance of mathematics. The damage and destruction done by history is twofold: firstly, it has tarnished the reputation regarding the compilation and completeness of the Quran, and secondly, it has intervened in creating new vowels, now placed within words, resulting in seemingly insignificant alterations, but has nonetheless caused considerable damage. We are determined to defeat the shadows of doubt and skepticism cast by historical narratives and to unveil the hidden mathematical connections and marvels within the Quran that will serve as our guiding light.

Simultaneously, we are confronted by the timeless challenge laid down by the Quran itself – a challenge that has echoed through the chronicles of history for over 1400 years. The challenge is about the composition and masterwork of the Quran; the challenge is to compose a single chapter similar to it. God, in His infinite wisdom, presents the challenge in several verses of the Quran, calling upon humanity to produce a book similar to the Quran, or even a single chapter like it:

(Quran 2:23) *"And if you are in doubt about what I have revealed to My servant [Muhammed], then produce* **one** *chapter like it, and call your witnesses besides God, if you are truthful."* **[75 Letters, 20 Words]**

(Quran 11:13) *"Or do they say, 'He has fabricated this (Quran)!'? Say, O Prophet, 'Produce* **ten** *chapters like it and seek help from whoever you can, other than God, if you are truthful!' "* **[77 Letters, 18 Words]**

(Quran 17:88) *"Say: 'Surely, if mankind and jinn were to get together to produce the like of this Quran, they will never be able to produce the like of it, no matter how they help one another.' "* **[76 Letters, 19 Words]**

Why is it such a formidable task to reproduce the likes of the Quran, or even compose a single chapter like it? Is it because of its eloquent literature, melodic poetry, or comprehensive coverage of topics? Or is it simply because the Quran has stood the test of time for over 1400 years without any alteration, variation, or version?

For the majority of Muslims, the Quran is revered as the mother of all Books, a miraculous revelation bestowed upon Prophet Muhammed (S) for all nations and all times. It is a testament to divine guidance and wisdom, transcending the bounds of human comprehension and defying replication. Its challenge has not been met and will always remain unchallenged.

In our quest to understand the intricacies of the Quran and its challenges, we must delve deeper into the essence of this divine revelation. The challenge to compose or produce anything comparable to the Quran goes beyond mere linguistic prowess or poetic eloquence. Possibly, the mathematical patterns and numerical symmetries woven into the text add another layer of complexity, reinforcing the argument that its composition is a masterpiece that is beyond human capability.

How is it that all three verses (2:23, 11:13, 17:88) that have been quoted, sharing the word *"mithle-hi"* ("like it"), also contain 77, 75, and 76 letters respectively, totaling 228, which is perfectly divisible by 19? And how do they, at the same time, hold 20, 18, and 19 words, totaling 57, again a perfect multiple of 19? Could such precision have arisen by chance? Is it merely a coincidence that the quoted chapter and verse numbers, when rearranged as 17882231311, would be a perfect multiple of 19? Could the "spontaneous" compilation be so well-structured and logical that the 2nd Chapter challenges the reader to produce just *one* chapter like it, while the 11th chapter calls to produce precisely *ten* chapters like it?

Could the Quran contain an inbuilt mathematical system that safeguards its integrity and perfection? Is this the divine code we seek to unravel – a code that will not only guide us in our quest to challenge history but also serve as a testament to the miraculous composition of the Quran itself?

Before we embark on this dual battle – to challenge history and understand the Quran's challenge – let us prepare our arsenal, sharpen our mathematical arrows, and fortify our understanding. In the upcoming chapters, we will delve directly into some fundamental mathematical concepts, familiarize ourselves with the Arabic alphabet, and gain a brief understanding of the Quran's structure, including its divisions, chapters, and verses.

By equipping ourselves with these essential tools, we will be better prepared to navigate the intricate pathways of the Quran's mathematical marvels and unlock the numerical code hidden within its verses. This foundational knowledge will serve as a compass that will navigate us towards the right route as we embark on this enlightening journey of exploration and discovery.

5

THE ARSENAL - ALPHABET, STRUCTURE, AND MATHEMATICS

To fight this battle, and in the pursuit of understanding the intricate mathematics embedded within the Quran, we embark on a journey that requires us to arm ourselves with formidable weapons. To effectively engage in this battle of comprehension, we must first familiarize ourselves with the infantry and cavalry that constitute our arsenal. Our main weapons, pivotal to our noble quest for enlightenment, are the Arabic Alphabet and its profound sequence, the existing structure of the Quran, and the fundamental concepts of Mathematics.

Arabic Alphabet

Our first fighting tool in this battle is exploring the Arabic Alphabet. Comprising 28 primary letters, with all other letters being modifications that did not exist in earlier scripts of the Holy Quran. The Arabic alphabet holds a crucial role in comprehending and deciphering the Quran's completeness and compilation.

Hija'i Alphabetical Order

Though there are several alphabetical orders in the Arabic language, one commonly taught and used representation of the Arabic alphabet is the *Hija'i* alphabetical order, illustrated in *chart 5.1*. The order number of each letter corresponds to its placement in the alphabet. For example, if ب is the second letter in the alphabet, its order number is 2. Similarly, if ن is the 25th letter, its order number is also 25.

It is important to investigate whether this order is the same one that God used when writing the Quran. In essence, we need to determine whether the *Hija'i* alphabetical order should also be considered a divine sequence.

HIJA'I ARABIC ALPHABET CHART

#1	ا	#8	د	#15	ض	#22	ك
#2	ب	#9	ذ	#16	ط	#23	ل
#3	ت	#10	ر	#17	ظ	#24	م
#4	ث	#11	ز	#18	ع	#25	ن
#5	ج	#12	س	#19	غ	#26	ه
#6	ح	#13	ش	#20	ف	#27	و
#7	خ	#14	ص	#21	ق	#28	ي

Chart 5.1

Dotted and Plain Letters

Additionally, out of the 28 Arabic letters, 15 have dots while 13 are plain, without dots. Later, we will see how the Quran balances the usage of dotted and undotted letters in various instances.

Vowels

It's crucial to acknowledge that history has already unleashed its weapons, particularly in the area of vowels. Vowel marks play a vital role in the Arabic language, as they can completely alter the meaning of a word. Generally, there are three short vowels in Arabic, the **'a'**, the **'i'** and the **'u'** (Fatha, *zabar* /a/ , Kasra, *zer* /i/, Damma/*pesh* /u/).

Fatha, *Zabar* /a/	بَ	**Ba**
Kasra, *Zer* /i/	بِ	**Bi**
Damma, *Pesh* /u/	بُ	**Bu**

Besides these three, there are two modern vowels – 'Hamza' (ء) and the short overhead vertical stroke over letters, called *dagger alif* (هٰ). Both of these are controversial, extensively used in the modern scripts of the Quran, requiring much attention.

'Hamza' (ء), the glottal stop that appears above or after certain Arabic letters, is not a distinct letter of the Arabic alphabet. Introduced in modern times, it was not used when the Quran was first written down. Therefore, it should only be considered a diacritical mark, not a letter of the alphabet.

Similarly, the *dagger alif* (هٰ), a diacritical mark that appears as a short vertical stroke on top of an Arabic letter, is not one of the 28 letters of the Arabic alphabet. It has replaced the original 'alif' or the long vowel 'alif' in many words, leaving a controversy. Its controversial usage has altered the letter count in certain words, affecting the Quran's textual structure. A few classic examples of these words are the dagger alif on *(Al-Aalamin)* ٱلْعَٰلَمِينَ [7 letters] vs. the original **الْعَالَمِينَ** [8 letters] and likewise, the dagger alif on *(Seerat)* صِرَٰطَ [3 letters] vs. the original **صِرَاطَ**

[4 letters], then the dagger alif on *(Maalik)* مَٰلِكِ [3 letters] vs. the original مَالِكِ [4 letters] and the dagger alif on *(Kitaab)* كِتَٰب [3 letters] vs. the original كِتَاب [4 letters]. We will discuss the dagger alif in greater detail in a separate chapter later in this book.

Structure of the Quran

Our next weapon in unraveling the mysteries of the Quran is to comprehend the Quran's structure as it exists today. The Holy Quran, a divine revelation in Arabic, was revealed upon the final Prophet Muhammed (S) by God over a span of 23 years through the archangel *Jibraeel* (Gabriel).

Surah is the term for a chapter, and *Ayah* is the term for a verse. The Quran is also divided into 30 parts, which are known as *Juz* or *Parah.*

Comprising **114** chapters or *surahs* of varying lengths, the Quran is a literary masterpiece, with some chapters being only a few lines long while others span several pages. The shortest chapter has only 3 lines, while the longest chapter has 286 lines. The Quran's official manuscript consists of **6236** verses or *ayah* and uses the Kufic numbering system for numbering its chapters and verses. Each verse in the Quran is assigned a mathematical value known as the verse number of that chapter. *Refer to Table 5.2,* which provides the names of all chapters along with their total verse counts. Chapters that contain *Muqattaat* (mysterious letters) are highlighted in grey. If poetry is defined by rhyming words, repetition, rhythm, and stanzas, then the Quran clearly displays these poetic qualities and is rightly considered as poetry.

When the Holy Quran is translated into other languages, it is referred to as a translation of the Holy Quran. However, it's important to note that only the original Arabic version of the Quran is recognized as the Holy Quran. Even if the Quran is transliterated into other scripts, the transliterated scripts are also not considered as the Holy Quran, but rather a transliteration of it.

The Quran has remained unchanged for over 1400 years, preserved in its original form without any alterations or versions, except for differences in Arabic scripts and styles. Additionally, a few new vowels have been introduced to assist non-native Arabic speakers in pronouncing the words accurately.

Covering a wide range of subjects, including physics, law, history, geography, biology, zoology, and botany, the Quran is a comprehensive religious text. Yet, beyond its linguistic brilliance and poetic distinction lies the question: Is the Quran also a mathematical miracle?

Header Of Chapters

بِسْمِ اللَّهِ الرَّحْمَٰنِ الرَّحِيمِ

"Bismillah Ar-Rahman Ar-Rahim"

(In the Name of God, the Gracious, the Merciful)

Remarkably, out of the 114 chapters, 112 begin with the unnumbered phrase "In the name of God, the Gracious, the Merciful" (*Bismillah Ar-Rahman Ar-Rahim*), comprising 19 letters. This phrase is the header of chapters and is not numbered. However, Chapter 1 includes this phrase as its first numbered verse and not as a header, and Chapter 9 does not have it at all, making both exceptions. These exceptional chapters, 1 and 9, without headers, form an intriguing pattern that leads us to a key mathematical clue – the number 19. There are 114 instances of the phrase *"Bismillah Ar-Rahman Ar-Rahim"* in the Quran. One of them is missing from Chapter 9 but can be found exactly 19 chapters away in Chapter 27, verse 30.

Structure Of The Holy Quran

Name	Chp #	Verses	Name	Chp #	Verses	Name	Chp #	Verses
Al-Fatiha	1	7	**Ta-Ha**	**20**	135	Az-Zumar	39	75
Al-Baqara	**2**	286	Al-Anbiya	21	112	**Al Mu'min**	**40**	85
Al-e-Imran	**3**	200	Al-Hajj	22	78	**Fussilat**	**41**	54
An-Nisa	4	176	Al-Muminoon	23	118	**Ash-Shura**	**42**	53
Al-Ma'ida	5	120	An-Nur	24	64	**Az-Zukhruf**	**43**	89
Al-An'am	6	165	Al-Furqan	25	77	**Ad-Dukhan**	**44**	59
Al-A'raf	**7**	206	**Ash-Shu'ara**	**26**	227	**Al-Jathiya**	**45**	37
Al-Anfal	8	75	**An-Naml**	**27**	93	**Al-Ahqaf**	**46**	35
At-Tawba	9	129	**Al-Qasas**	**28**	88	Muhammad	47	38
Yunus	**10**	109	**Al-Ankabut**	**29**	69	Al-Fath	48	29
Hud	**11**	123	**Ar-Rum**	**30**	60	Al-Hujurat	49	18
Yusuf	**12**	111	**Luqman**	**31**	34	**Qaf**	**50**	45
Ar-Ra'd	**13**	43	**As-Sajda**	**32**	30	Adh-Dhariyat	51	60
Ibrahim	**14**	52	Al-Ahzab	33	73	At-Tur	52	49
Al-Hijr	**15**	99	Saba	34	54	An-Najm	53	62
An-Nahl	16	128	Al-Mala'ikah	35	45	Al-Qamar	54	55
Al-Isra	17	111	**Ya Sin**	**36**	83	Ar-Rahman	55	78
Al-Kahf	18	110	As-Saaffat	37	182	Al-Waqi'a	56	96
Maryam	**19**	98	**Saad**	**38**	88	Al-Hadid	57	29
							1653	**5104**

- HALF -

Name	Chp #	Verses	Name	Chp #	Verses	Name	Chp #	Verses
Al-Mujadila	58	22	Al-Mursalat	77	50	Al-Alaq	96	19
Al-Hashr	59	24	An-Naba	78	40	Al-Qadr	97	5
Al-Mumtahina	60	13	An-Naziat	79	46	Al-Bayyina	98	8
As-Saff	61	14	Abasa	80	42	Az-Zalzala	99	8
Al-Jumah	62	11	At-Takwir	81	29	Al-Adiyat	100	11
Al-Munafiqun	63	11	Al-Infitar	82	19	Al-Qaria	101	11
At-Taghabun	64	18	Al-Mutaffifin	83	36	At-Takathur	102	8
At-Talaq	65	12	Al-Inshiqaq	84	25	Al-Asr	103	3
At-Tahrim	66	12	Al-Burooj	85	22	Al-Humaza	104	9
Al-Mulk	67	30	At-Tariq	86	17	Al-Fil	105	5
Al-Qalam	**68**	52	Al-'Ala	87	19	Quraysh	106	4
Al-Haaqqa	69	52	Al-Ghashiya	88	26	Al-Ma'un	107	7
Al-Maarij	70	44	Al-Fajr	89	30	Al-Kawthar	108	3
Nuh	71	28	Al-Balad	90	20	Al-Kafirun	109	6
Al-Jinn	72	28	Ash-Shams	91	15	An-Nasr	110	3
Al-Muzzammil	73	20	Al-Lail	92	21	Al-Masadd	111	5
Al-Muddathir	74	56	Ad-Dhuha	93	11	Al-Ikhlas	112	4
Al-Qiyama	75	40	Al-Inshirah	94	8	Al-Falaq	113	5
Al-Insan	76	31	At-Tin	95	8	Al-Naas	114	6
							6555	**6236**

Table 5.2 *(Chapters containing Muqattaat are highlighted in grey)*

Hurouf Al-Muqattaat

As we delve deeper into our quest for mathematical codes and correlations within the Quran, we encounter another enigma in the structure of the Quran – *Al Hurouf Al-Muqattaat*, also known as Separated Letters or Mysterious Letters.

In total, there are 30 *Muqattaat,* which are found at the beginning of 29 chapters. These letters are a combination of 14 Arabic letters.

In the chapters to come, we will explore these mysterious letters in greater detail, uncovering their significance in the divine tapestry of the Quran's structure.

Fundamentals of Mathematics

Before we start exploring the mathematical intricacies embedded within the Quran, it is essential to acquaint ourselves with basic mathematical concepts. Apart from the elementary operations of addition, subtraction, multiplication, and division, there are several other mathematical concepts that we need to acquaint ourselves with. Additionally, we must also explore two important numbers explicitly mentioned in the Quran. These will serve as our most important weapons as we embark on our exploration.

Natural numbers

Natural numbers are all positive integers starting from 1 to infinity. They can be further divided into two main categories: prime and composite numbers.

Unit (1) - One

A unit (1) is a fundamental natural number that stands alone and cannot be divided further. It represents the smallest natural number and refers to a single numerical digit. As it cannot be divided or split by any other number except itself, number 1 is not considered prime. 1 is a unique number.

Prime numbers

Prime numbers are called the "building blocks" of mathematics because all natural numbers can be expressed as products of prime numbers. Prime numbers are unique numbers greater than 1 that can only be divided or split by 1 and themselves without leaving a remainder. They have no factors other than 1 and themselves. Prime numbers play a crucial role in various mathematical applications, particularly in cryptography, where they are used as the foundation for secure communication. The first 10 examples of prime numbers are 2, 3, 5, 7, 11, 13, 17, 19, 23, and 29. Distinctly, 19 is the 8th Prime number.

Composite numbers

Composite numbers are natural numbers with more than two factors and are not prime numbers. They can be divided evenly by numbers other than 1 and themselves. The first 19 examples of composite numbers are 4, 6, 8, 9, 10, 12, 14, 15, 16, 18, 20, 21, 22, 24, 25, 26, 27, 28, and 30. Notably, 30 is the 19th Composite number.

Mirror numbers

Mirror numbers are the reversed forms of a number, where the digits are mirrored. They can be symmetrical, like 55 and 55 or 151 and 151 or 1001 and 1001, which read the same from left to right and right to left, or asymmetrical, like 13 and 31, 63 and 36, 411 and 114.
In the Arabic language, text is read from right to left while numbers are read from left to right. This unique characteristic creates a mirrored appearance for Arabic numbers within text lines. It appears as if the number is the mirror image of itself. *For example:*

English		**Arabic**
Road number 139	*is written as*	رقم الطريق ١٣٩

Left to Right	(Words)	*Right to Left*
Left to Right	(Numbers)	*Left to Right*

In the following discussion, we will explore the significance of two specific numbers in the Quran: 7 and 19. These numbers hold great importance in Islam and are closely connected to many aspects of the Quran and the creation of the Universe.

Number 7

Number 7 is a prime number and holds symbolic importance in Islamic teachings. In the decimal number system, 7 is the only digit that has neither parent nor child. For instance, 3 could have 9 as its parent, and 2 could be considered the child of 4. However, 7 stands alone in the decimal system.

Here are some examples of the significance of the number 7 within the Quran, Islam, and Nature.

- The first chapter of the Quran, *Al-Fateha*, consists of 7 verses, which are also referred to as "the seven often-repeated verses" in Chapter 15:87
- The first prostration *(Sajda)* verse in the Quran is found in Chapter 7 at 7:206.
- The first number mentioned in the Quran is 7 (*Saba*) in Chapter 2:29.
- The Quran mentions the creation of 7 skies and 7 firmaments throughout the book.
- There are 7 gates of Hell mentioned in Chapter 15:44

- Performing circumambulation *(Tawaf)* around the Holy Kaaba involves completing 7 rounds, and the symbolic stoning of Satan during Haj is done by throwing 7 stones at each of the three pillars.
- Only 7 Chapters of the Quran (18, 35, 48, 52, 71, 92, 110) start and end with the same letter.
- During prostration in prayer, Muslims touch the ground with 7 parts of their body – both hands, knees, feet, and forehead.
- The human neck is said to contain 7 bones.
- There are 7 days in a week.
- There are 7 pure notes in sound
- The white light, made up of 7 colors, can be seen in a rainbow.

Number 19

Number 19 is also a prime number and holds special significance in the Quran. Let us see the essence of this unique number through a few mathematical expressions and concepts.

✓ The number 19 can be expressed as the sum of 10 and 9. Mathematically, this is represented as:

$$(10 + 9) \textit{ or } [(10)^1 + (9)^1] = \mathbf{19}$$
$$\textit{Hence the equation } (x^1 + y^1) = \mathbf{19}$$

✓ The number 19 can also be expressed as the difference of the squares of 10 and 9. This is shown Mathematically as:

$$(10)^2 - (9)^2 = (100 - 81) = \mathbf{19}$$
$$\textit{Hence the equation } (x^2 - y^2) = \mathbf{19}$$

✓ The sum of all the numbers up to 19 equals ten times the number, which is 190, as:

$$(1+2+3+4+5+6+7+8+9+10+11+12+13+14+15+16+17+18+19) = \mathbf{190}$$

✓ Each human hand has 19 bones in the palm.

In the context of the Quran, the number 19 acts as the sign and the seal of the sacred text. Just like a document is considered finished and official because it is signed and sealed, many examples and arguments in the Quran are concluded with the number 19. The Quran points out the significance of the number 19, without giving much detail, in the following verse :

عَلَيْهَا تِسْعَةَ عَشَرَ ۝

"Over it are Nineteen" (74: 30)

Some examples of the significance of number 19 within the Quran:

- The first verse of the Quran (1:1) reads بِسْمِ ٱللَّهِ ٱلرَّحْمَـٰنِ ٱلرَّحِيمِ *"In the Name of God, the Gracious, the Merciful"*. This verse contains **19** letters, meaning that the Quran begins with 19 letters.

19 Letters

6	6	4	3
الرَّحِيمِ	الرَّحْمَـٰنِ	اللَّهِ	بِسْمِ

- The total number of chapters in the Quran is **114**, which is a multiple of 19 (19 x 6).
- The total number of occurrences of the phrase *"In the Name of God, the Gracious, the Merciful"* in the Quran is **114** (19 x 6).
- The 96th Chapter of the Quran, *Surah Al-Alaq,* was the first chapter to be revealed. At the start of the revelation, its 5 lines, consisting of **19** words, were revealed. The chapter contains **19** verses and is also the 19th Chapter when counted backwards from the 114th Chapter.

- First line of chapter 48, Al-Fath (48:1) إِنَّا فَتَحْنَا لَكَ فَتْحًا مُّبِينًا *[Inna Fatahna laka Fatham Mubeena]* meaning (Indeed, We have granted you a clear victory) contains **19** letters.
- The placements of the two most renowned chapters of the Quran are Chapter 36, *Ya-Seen,* and Chapter 48, *Al Fath.* The appended number **3648** is perfectly divisible by 19. Another renowned chapter is 55, Ar-*Rahman.* In light of Chapter 36 and 48, the appended number **5548** is also divisible by 19 and the difference between chapter numbers (55 - 36) is exactly19.
- There are exactly **19** chapters in the Quran that have less than 10 verses. The number of verses in these 19 Chapters is a single digit, and they do not reach double digits. The list of these 19 chapters is as follows: (1, 94, 95, 97, 98, 99, 102, 103, 104, 105, 106, 107, 108, 109, 110, 111, 112, 113, 114).
- The most repeated chapter length in the Quran is either 8 or 11 verses. Both are equally balanced, five chapters (94, 95, 98, 99, 102), have 8 verses, and the other five chapters (62, 63, 93, 100, 101) have 11 verses. Again, the sum of 8 and 11 is **19**.

The following are a few examples of the results of appending numbers and uncovering the significance of the number 19:

- The Quran begins with a chapter *(Surah Al-Fateha)* with 7 lines and ends with a chapter *(Surah An-Nas)* with 6 lines. When their digits are appended or combined, we get (**76**), a multiple of 19 (19 x 4).
- In the last Chapter (114) of the Quran, Line 1 contains 14 letters. When both these digits are appended, we get (**114**), a multiple of 19 (19 x 6).
- The last line of the Quran contains 13 letters and 3 words. When both these digits are appended or combined, we get (**133**), again a multiple of 19 (19 x 7).

Continuing our discussion on the significance of the number 19, let us uncover more fascinating connections:

- Muslims are supposed to pray 5 times a day, from early morning to night in specific units (2, 4, 4, 3, 4), totalling 17 units. The appended sequence of these units is 24434, which is a multiple of 19, since **24434 = (19 x 1286).**
- The 5 names of the *Ahlul-Bait* combined contain 19 letters:

  19 Letters — محمد (4) على (3) فاطمه (5) حسن (3) حسين (4)

  As mentioned, the first verse of the Quran also contains 19 letters:

  19 Letters — بِسْمِ (3) اللَّهِ (4) الرَّحْمَٰنِ (6) الرَّحِيمِ (6)

  The surprising fact is that the numbers generated from both the phrases 43534 and 6643 are not divisible by 19. However, when these numbers are reversed and combined, they form **435343466**, which is perfectly divisible by 19.
- The word "*Qaaba*" **كعبة** consists of 4 Arabic letters **(ب ع ك ة)**. Their positions in the alphabet chart are 2, 18, 22, and 26. Their combined number 2182226 is a perfect multiple of 19.

In the forthcoming chapters, we will also unravel the Golden Ratio and the Fibonacci sequence within the Quran. However, our immediate focus remains on comprehending the mathematical codes and correlations embedded in the Quran, led by the numbers 7 and 19.

Let us now embark on the journey of exploration, armed with mathematical fundamentals and a deep understanding of the Quran's structure. Together, we will unveil the hidden correlations concealed within the Quran's verses and unlock one of the biggest challenges of the Quran.

6

THE PERFECTLY BALANCED BOOK

Two mighty warriors stand poised for combat on the battleground: Mathematics and History. Each revered in their own right, wielding formidable weapons of truth and insight. Yet, their paths were destined to clash over the enigmatic text of the Quran.

As the battle lines are drawn, Mathematics steps forward, armed with various numbers, patterns, and proofs. Its goal is clear: to demonstrate that the Quran was not merely a historical artifact but a meticulously crafted masterpiece, encoded with mathematical precision that surpasses human capability.

As our quest to unravel the mysteries of the Quran continues, we find ourselves confronted with a profound question: Was the Quran compiled by man or God? Was the Quran compiled as history narrates it, or was it divinely compiled? This question lies at the heart of our exploration as we seek to understand the authenticity and integrity of the Quranic structure.

The Perfect Odd and Even Distribution 57:57

One aspect of the Quran that piques our curiosity is its unique structure, particularly the distribution of chapters and verses. At first glance, it may appear there are more chapters with odd verses than even verses. With a total of 114 chapters, there are 60 chapters with odd verses and 54 chapters with even verses. However, upon closer examination, we discover a fascinating pattern that challenges our preconceptions.

Upon changing our perspective and with thorough analysis, we realize that the Quran can be split into an equal number of odd and even chapters. If we add the number of verses in each chapter to its chapter number (Chapter No. + Total Verses of that Chapter), we get a perfect balance: 57 odd chapters and 57 even chapters. For instance, if Chapter No. 1 has 7 verses, adding them together gives us 8, an even number. Similarly, Chapter No. 3 with 200 verses totals 203, an odd number, and so on for all the chapters. *Refer to Table 6.1*

The precision of the odd-even split within the Quran extends even further when we look into the specific numbers involved. The **57:57** ratio of odd-numbered chapters to even-numbered chapters is important as 57 is also a multiple of 19. In our search, we will stumble upon this significant ratio again. This ratio is significant because, if the Quran is divided into two halves based on its 114 chapters, we still obtain the 57:57 ratio. Not only do we observe an equal number of chapters with odd and even verses, but we also discover a remarkable correlation in the numerical values associated with these chapters.

What is even more remarkable is that the sum of all the even-numbered chapters in the Quran is precisely **6236**, which equals the total number of verses in the Quran. Similarly, the sum of all the odd-numbered chapters in the Quran is **6555**, equivalent to the sum of all numbers from 1 to 114 in Mathematics.

Upon closer examination, we find that 6 numbers on the even side of the Quran's distribution are divisible by 19. These numbers, when summed up, yield a total of **722**. These numbers are 114, 114, 152, 114, 114, and 114. *(Refer to Table 6.1)*

Chapter Number + Total Verses							
	EVEN				**ODD**		
Sr. No.	***1*** *-to-* ***19***	***20*** *-to-* ***38***	***39*** *-to-* ***57***	**UNSORTED**	***58*** *-to-* ***76***	***77*** *-to-* ***95***	***96*** *-to-* ***114***
	8	106	110		203	81	115
	288	88	106		125	85	107
	180	80	**114**		**171**	77	127
	138	126	110		213	67	125
	134	**114**	106		83	**95**	101
	56	132	104		119	111	119
	66	82	102		123	101	109
	114	**152**	102		117	115	107
	144	86	106		155	109	103
	128	80	112		**133**	**133**	119
	128	74	110		141	83	113
	100	82	106		253	73	103
	88	78	110		65	75	115
	102	120	110		119	73	107
	120	**114**	**114**		219	77	111
	116	100	116		125	97	113
	98	130	116		**95**	121	111
	90	118	118		**95**	99	115
	62	122	120		103	93	113

⇒	EVEN Chapters = **57**	ODD Chapters = **57**	⇐
⇒	Sum of Ch. Nos. = **6236**	Sum of Ch. Nos. = **6555**	⇐
⇒	Divisible by ÷ 19 = **6 Chp.**	Divisible by ÷ 19 = **6 Chp.**	⇐
⇒	**Σ 6** Chapters Nos. = **722**	**Σ 6** Chapters Nos. = **722**	⇐

Table 6.1

Similarly, on the odd side of the distribution, we encounter another set of 6 numbers divisible by 19. Once again, the sum of these numbers amounts to 722. These numbers are 171, 133, 95, 95, 95, and 133. *(Refer to Table 6.1)*

The fact that both sets of 6 numbers add up to the same total 722 underscores the meticulous design and precise arrangement of the Quranic text. This intricate numerical pattern not only reinforces the symmetry between odd and even chapters but also highlights the profound mathematical harmony embedded within the Quran.

* * *

The Perfect Start and End 24:24

Another fascinating aspect of the Quran's intricate structure lies in the balanced use of letters that start and end its chapters. There is a total of 48 different combinations in the Quran that define the starting and ending letters of its chapters. The perfect balance is reflected in the unique combinations of starting and ending letters of chapters and repeated combinations of letters that start and end the chapters. *(Refer to Table 6.2)*

Specifically, there are **24** unique combinations of starting and ending letters, each forming 24 distinct chapters. These combinations stand alone, with no repetition across other chapters.

In parallel to these unique combinations, there are exactly **24** combinations that are repeated and collectively form 90 chapters. This duality of 24 unique and 24 repeated combinations further highlights the symmetry and balance within the Quran.

Start and End Letters of Chapters

Count	Ch. No.	**Unique** Combination	Count	**Repeat** Combination	No. of Ch.
#1	1	ب ن	#1	ا ن	16
#2	9	ب م	#2	ى م	4
#3	19	ك ا	#3	ى ر	3
#4	20	ط ى	#4	ا م	6
#5	25	ت ا	#5	ا ب	5
#6	38	ص ن	#6	س ا	2
#7	41	ح ط	#7	ا ا	5
#8	42	ح ر	#8	ق ن	3
#9	45	ح م	#9	س م	3
#10	68	ن ن	#10	ط ن	3
#11	72	ق ا	#11	ا ر	4
#12	74	ى ه	#12	ى ا	2
#13	76	ه ا	#13	ى ن	4
#14	78	ع ا	#14	و ن	5
#15	80	ع ه	#15	ت ن	2
#16	85	و ظ	#16	ح ن	4
#17	87	ه ى	#17	ق د	3
#18	92	ى ى	#18	و م	2
#19	93	و ث	#19	و ا	3
#20	98	ل ه	#20	س ن	2
#21	105	ا ل	#21	ل ى	2
#22	106	ل ف	#22	ا ه	3
#23	111	ت د	#23	و ه	2
★ **#24**	114	ق س	**#24**	و ر	2
24				**TOTAL**	**90**

Table 6.2

To add an extra dimension, out of the 24 unique combinations, two chapters are exceptional: Chapter 68 begins with "**ن**" and ends with "**ن**", and Chapter 92 begins with "**ي**" and ends with "**ي**". These combinations are not repeated elsewhere. The difference between the chapter numbers (92 - 68) also equals **24**.

Probing deeper into letters that start and end chapters, we find another consistency, that of number 7:

- The number of combinations that begin with the letter *"alif"* (أ) is precisely **7**.

Count	1	2	3	4	5	6	7
Start أ	ال	ان	ام	اب	اا	ار	اه

- Similarly, there are **7** chapters where the starting and ending letters of a chapter are the same.

Chapter No.	68	92	18	35	48	71	110
Combinations	ن ن	ى ى	ا ا	ا ا	ا ا	ا ا	ا ا
Count	1	2	3	4	5	6	7

- The total number of letters used for starting and ending the chapters is **21**. So, the number of letters not used as starting or ending letters is precisely 7.

Count	1	2	3	4	5	6	7
Not Used	غ	ظ	ش	ز	ذ	خ	ج

As we continue our exploration, we are left in awe of the meticulous craftsmanship that underlies the Quran's structure. Each chapter, each verse, and each numerical value has been carefully orchestrated, reflecting a purpose and a pattern that is beyond human comprehension.

This mathematical pattern offers profound insights into the compilation of the Quran. Even a slight alteration of adding or removing a verse could potentially disrupt the delicate balance between odd and even chapters or the balance between the start and end letters.

* * *

The Perfect Anchors: Chapter 57 & Chapter 1

In the vast ocean of the Quran's mathematical composition, two chapters emerge as unwavering anchors: Chapter 1 and Chapter 57. These two chapters, in conjunction with their number of verses, are positioned at critical points within the structure of the Quran. Their mathematical behavior remains unchanged, acting as fixed points in a seemingly fluid system, reinforcing the idea that the Quran's composition follows a preordained design.

The Anchor - Chapter 57

Chapter 57, known as Surah Al-Hadid, contains 29 verses and is positioned at the exact midpoint of the Quran. With 114 chapters in total, Chapter 57 divides the Quran into two halves. Notably, 57 is a multiple of 19. The end of Chapter 57 also marks the end of the 27th *Juz (Para)* of the Quran. This indicates that half of the Quran is contained in 27 *Juz (Para)* while the remaining half is in 3 *Juz (Para)*. In terms of ratio, the Quran is divided into 3:27 *Juz*. This ratio can also be expressed as **1:9** mathematically, which is another pointer to the number 19.

If we take each chapter number of the Quran and multiply it by the number of verses it contains, and then arrange the results in ascending order, an astonishing pattern emerges. Amidst this arrangement, Chapter 57, when multiplied by its 29 verses, results in **1653**, which remains at the center, at the 57th position, unmoved by any fluctuation in the sequence, despite sorting all the numbers in ascending order. It behaves as an anchor - no matter how the sequence is manipulated in ascending or descending order, it holds firm in its position, reinforcing the idea that this chapter was destined to serve as the central pillar of the divine composition. *Refer to Table 6.3 and compare it to Table 5.2*

Chapter No. and its Verses - MULTIPLIED and SORTED

Name	Chp. No.	Σ Vrs.	(Chp x Vrs.)
Al-Fatiha	**1**	**7**	**7**
Al-Asr	103	3	309
Al-Kawthar	108	3	324
An-Nasr	110	3	330
Quraysh	106	4	424
Al-Ikhlas	112	4	448
Al-Qadr	97	5	485
Al-Fil	105	5	525
Al-Masadd	111	5	555
Ar-Ra'd	13	43	559
Al-Falaq	113	5	565
Al-Baqara	2	286	572
Al-i-Imran	3	200	600
Al-Ma'ida	5	120	600
Al-Anfal	8	75	600
Al-Kafirun	109	6	654
Al-Jumuah	62	11	682
Al-Nas	114	6	684
Al-Munafiqun	63	11	693

Name	Ch. No.	Σ Vrs.	(Chp x Vrs.)
An-Nisa	4	176	704
Ibrahim	14	52	728
Al-Ma'un	107	7	749
Al-Inshirah	94	8	752
At-Tin	95	8	760
Al-Mumtahina	60	13	780
At-Talaq	65	12	780
Al-Bayyina	98	8	784
At-Tahrim	66	12	792
Az-Zalzala	99	8	792
At-Takathur	102	8	816
As-Saff	61	14	854
Al-Hujurat	49	18	882
Al-Humaza	104	9	936
As-Sajda	32	30	960
Al-An'am	6	165	990
Ad-Dhuha	93	11	1023
Luqman	31	34	1054
Yunus	10	109	1090

Name	Ch. No.	Σ Vrs.	(Chp x Vrs.)
Al-Adiyat	100	11	1100
Al-Qaria	101	11	1111
At-Taghabun	64	18	1152
At-Tawba	9	129	1161
Al-Mujadila	58	22	1276
Yusuf	12	111	1332
Hud	11	123	1353
Ash-Shams	91	15	1365
Al-Fath	48	29	1392
Al-Hashr	59	24	1416
Al-A'raf	7	206	1442
Al-Muzzammil	73	20	1460
At-Tariq	86	17	1462
Al-Hijr	15	99	1485
An-Nur	24	64	1536
Al-Infitar	82	19	1558
Al-Mala'ikah	35	45	1575
Al-Ahqaf	46	35	1610
Al-Hadid	**57**	**29**	**1653**

- HALF -

Name	Ch. No.	Σ Vrs.	(Chp x Vrs.)
Al-'Ala	87	19	1653
Al-Jathiya	45	37	1665
Al-Hajj	22	78	1716
Muhammad	47	38	1786
Ar-Rum	30	60	1800
Al-Balad	90	20	1800
Al-Alaq	96	19	1824
Saba	34	54	1836
Maryam	19	98	1862
Al-Burooj	85	22	1870
Al-Isra	17	111	1887
Al-Furqan	25	77	1925
Al-Lail	92	21	1932
Al-Kahf	18	110	1980
Nuh	71	28	1988
Al-Ankabut	29	69	2001
Al-Mulk	67	30	2010
Al-Jinn	72	28	2016
An-Nahl	16	128	2048

Name	Ch. No.	Σ Vrs.	(Chp x Vrs.)
Al-Inshiqaq	84	25	2100
Fussilat	41	54	2214
Ash-Shura	42	53	2226
Qaf	50	45	2250
Al-Ghashiya	88	26	2288
At-Takwir	81	29	2349
Al-Anbiya	21	112	2352
Al-Insan	76	31	2356
Al-Ahzab	33	73	2409
Al-Qasas	28	88	2464
An-Naml	27	93	2511
At-Tur	52	49	2548
Ad-Dukhan	44	59	2596
Al-Fajr	89	30	2670
Ta-Ha	20	135	2700
Al-Muminoon	23	118	2714
Az-Zumar	39	75	2925
Al-Qamar	54	55	2970
Ya Sin	36	83	2988

Name	Ch. No.	Σ Vrs.	(Chp x Vrs.)
Al-Mutaffifin	83	36	2988
Al-Qiyama	75	40	3000
Adh-Dhariyat	51	60	3060
Al-Maarij	70	44	3080
An-Naba	78	40	3120
An-Najm	53	62	3286
Sad	38	88	3344
Abasa	80	42	3360
Al Mu'min	40	85	3400
Al-Qalam	68	52	3536
Al-Haaqqa	69	52	3588
An-Naziat	79	46	3634
Az-Zukhruf	43	89	3827
Al-Mursalat	77	50	3850
Al-Muddathir	74	56	4144
Ar-Rahman	55	78	4290
Al-Waqi'a	56	96	5376
Ash-Shu'ara	26	227	5902
As-Saaffat	37	182	6734

Table 6.3

Special Note: *There are only two chapters in the Quran with 29 verses: Chapter 57:29 and Chapter 81:29. Interestingly, their combined number, 57298129, is a perfect multiple of 19.*

The Anchor - Chapter 1

Just as Chapter 57 is the anchor at the center, Chapter 1 (Surah Al-Fateha) is the robust anchor at the very beginning. If we apply the same principle as before, multiplying each chapter number by its number of verses and sorting the results in ascending order. Chapter 1, when multiplied by its 7 verses, results in 7, and stays at the start of the list, maintaining its 1st position and significance. Chapter 1 does not change its starting position, just as Chapter 57 remains at the center. *Refer to Table 6.3 and compare it to Table 5.2.*

This dual anchoring system - one at the start and one at the center - ensures balance and symmetry within the Quran's compilation. Chapter 1 serves as the beginning foundation, while Chapter 57 acts as the middle stabilizer, keeping the entire structure intact.

In light of this, we are compelled to reconsider the process of Quranic compilation. Could it be that the Quran was compiled under divine guidance, ensuring the preservation of its numerical integrity? The Quran itself alludes to this possibility, with Almighty God stating,

"It is for Us to gather it and to relate (correlate) it" (75:17).

This prompts us to search deeper into the mathematical intricacies of the Quran, exploring further examples to ascertain the veracity of its preservation. Our journey into the mathematical marvels of the Quran has only just begun, and we are eager to uncover more revelations that lie hidden within its sacred verses.

7

THE FUSION OF MATHEMATICS AND THE QURAN

For centuries, History has told its tales, chronicling events and interpretations with an authoritative voice. But Mathematics, with its precise and unyielding logic, has begun to whisper a different story - a story of divine intelligence woven into the very fabric of the Quran.

When exploring the deep interconnections between mathematics and the Quran, we discover a remarkable fusion of mathematical concepts intricately woven into the fabric of divine revelation. Through meticulous analysis and scrutiny, we uncover the seamless integration of mathematical concepts within the structural framework of the Quran, surpassing mere coincidence to reveal a profound design infused with numerical elegance.

At first glance, the Quran might appear to be a straightforward collection of verses and chapters. However, a closer examination reveals a complex structure underpinned by mathematical principles. These principles are not random but are meticulously integrated, pointing to a profound and deliberate design.

The Square Numbers

One of the fascinating aspects of the Quran's numerical structure is the use of square numbers. A square number is the result of multiplying a number by itself. For example, 5 x 5 = 25, so 25 is a square number or 7 x 7 = 49, which is a square number.

Let us list down all the chapter numbers from 1 to 114 which are a square number in Example A *(Refer to Table 7.1)*

Let us also list down in Example B all the chapter numbers where the difference between the chapter number and its total verses is a square number. *(Refer to Table 7.1)*

Square Numbers

Example A

√	C		V
1^2	1	:	7
2^2	4	:	176
3^2	9	:	129
4^2	16	:	128
5^2	25	:	77
6^2	36	:	83
7^2	49	:	18
8^2	64	:	18
9^2	81	:	29
10^2	100	:	11
26^2			**676**

⇒ $676 = (26)^2$

⇒ $6+7+6 =$ **19**

$361 = (19)^2$ ⇐

Example B

C		V	C- V	√
47	:	38	9	3^2
58	:	22	36	6^2
68	:	52	16	4^2
103	:	3	100	10^2
105	:	5	100	10^2
107	:	7	100	10^2
TOTAL :			**361**	**19^2**

Table 7.1

Example A: Within the sacred chapters of the Quran, we encounter 10 chapters whose chapter numbers stand as perfect square numbers: 1, 4, 9, 16, 25, 36, 49, 64, 81, and 100. Upon closer examination, we observe that the sum of the total number of verses in these chapters, namely 7, 176, 129, 128, 77, 83, 18, 18, 29, and 11, respectively, yields a square number **676**, the square of 26. Notably, the digits of this square number (6+7+6) sum to 19, unveiling a fascinating numerical harmony. The number 19 acts as the sign and the seal of the sacred text.

Example B: Additionally, within the Quran lie six chapters wherein the difference between the chapter number and verse number forms perfect square numbers: 9, 36, 16, 100, 100, and 100. Intriguingly, the cumulative sum of these square numbers from the six chapters amounts to another square number, **361**, a perfect square of 19.

The Cube Numbers

The presence of cube numbers adds another layer of complexity and sophistication to the miraculous text of the Quran. A cube number is the result of multiplying a number by itself twice. For example, 3 x 3 x 3 = 27, so 27 is a cube number or 7 x 7 x 7 = 343, a cube number

Let us list down all the chapter numbers from 1 to 114 whose verses are cube numbers in Example A. *(Refer to Table 7.2)*

Let us also list down in Example B all the chapter numbers where the sum of the chapter number and its total verses is a cube number. *(Refer to Table 7.2)*

Cube Numbers

Example A

C		V	$\sqrt[3]{}$
24	:	64	4^3
94	:	8	2^3
95	:	8	2^3
98	:	8	2^3
99	:	8	2^3
102	:	8	2^3
512		**104**	

⇒ $512 = (8^3)$

⇒ $(5+1+2) = 8 = (2^3)$

Example B

C		V	C + V	$\sqrt[3]{}$
1	:	7	8	2^3
5	:	120	125	5^3
40	:	85	125	5^3
79	:	46	125	5^3
125		**258**		

⇒ $125 = (5^3)$

⇒ $(1+2+5) = 8 = (2^3)$

Table 7.2

Example A: Probing deeper into the numerical intricacies, we find six chapters in the Quran whose total verses correspond to cube numbers: 64, 8, 8, 8, 8, and 8, respectively. Astonishingly, the summation of the chapter numbers of these chapters, namely 24, 94, 95, 98, 99, and 102, yields a cube number **512**, which is a cube of 8. Notably, the digits of this cube number (5+1+2) also sum to 8. It should also be noted that 8 itself is the cube of 2, further emphasizing the mathematical elegance embedded within the Quran.

Example B: Four chapters exhibit the remarkable property wherein the sum of the chapter number and verse number equals cube numbers: 8, 125, 125, and 125, respectively. Upon meticulous examination, the cumulative sum of their corresponding chapter numbers, namely 1, 5, 40, and 79, astonishingly amounts to another cube number **125**, which is the cube of 5. Moreover, the digits of this cube number (1+2+5) also sum to 8, the cube of 2. Again and again, the profound mathematical coherence within the Quran is emphasized.

The Numbers Divisible by 19

One of the most striking mathematical marvels in the Quran is the number 19. This number recurs in various forms and contexts throughout the text. The total number of chapters, the arrangement of verses, the structure of specific words, and the occurrence of certain letters all show a remarkable alignment with the number 19. This recurrence is not random but rather a clear indication of a deliberate design. That is why it is referred to as the sign and the seal of the Quran.

Let us list down all the chapters where the sum or difference of the chapter number and its total verses is perfectly divisible by 19. *Refer to Table 7.3*

Perfectly Divisible by (÷) 19

Example A (Sum ÷ 19)

	C		V	C + V
#1	6	:	165	171
#2	15	:	99	114
#3	21	:	112	133
#4	39	:	75	114
#5	41	:	54	95
#6	42	:	53	95
#7	50	:	45	95
#8	55	:	78	133
#9	56	:	96	152
#10	70	:	44	114
#11	88	:	26	114
#12	107	:	7	114
Σ	590		854	1444

Example B (Difference ÷ 19)

	C		V	C - V
#1	14	:	52	38
#2	23	:	118	95
#3	48	:	29	19
#4	78	:	40	38
#5	80	:	42	38
#6	91	:	15	76
#7	104	:	9	95
Σ	438		305	399

⇒ Total = (#12 + #7) = **#19**

⇒ (Σ 590 - Σ 438) = 152 (÷ 19)

⇒ (Σ 854 + Σ 305) = 1159 (÷ 19)

Table 7.3

Example A: The Quran unveils 12 chapters wherein the sum of the chapter number and its total verses is perfectly divisible by 19. Upon summation, the chapter numbers equal 590 and the related verse numbers equal 854. *Nothing remarkable here!*

Example B: Similarly, 7 chapters are seen wherein the difference between the chapter number and verse number is divisible by 19. Upon summation of the chapter numbers and related verse numbers, we arrive at the sum of 438 and 305, respectively. *Nothing amazing here too!*

What is remarkable and amazing is that by combining the results of Example A with Example B *(Refer to Table 7.3),* we unveil fascinating observations that show a noteworthy affiliation with the number 19 and underscore the profound unity of mathematical principles within the Quran:

- The total number of chapters from Example A and B (12 +7) is equal to **19** chapters.
- The difference between the sum of chapter numbers from Example A and B (590 - 438) is **152**, which is divisible by 19.
- The sum of verse numbers from Example A and B (854 + 305) is **1159**, which is also divisible by 19.

19 Verses in Chapters

- Another interesting symmetry to note is that the chapters in the Quran having a minimum of 19 verses are a total of 82. Strikingly, Chapter 82 contains exactly 19 verses.

- Additionally, except for Chapter 1, from Chapter 2 to Chapter 48, 47 chapters continuously feature 19 verses each. Distinctively, Chapter 47 has 38 verses, which is a multiple of 19.

- Finally, there is one more significant section from Chapter 67 to Chapter 85, which continuously has a minimum of 19 verses in them, and which are exactly 19 chapters in continuation. *Refer to Table 5.2*

Verse Number 19 with 19 Words

- Chapter 2, verse 19, and Chapter 34, verse 19 are two verses in the Quran that are both numbered 19 and contain 19 words. Out of 6236 lines in the Quran, the position of these verses is the 26th line and the 3625th line, respectively. Appending both of these numbers, results in **263625**, which is a perfect multiple of 19.

- The verse with the highest word count is Chapter 2, Verse 282, which contains 128 words. Conversely, the first verse with the lowest word count is Chapter 2, Verse 1, consisting of only 1 word. Calculating the difference between their combined numerical references (2282 for Chapter 2:282, and 21 for Chapter 2:1), we find that (2282 - 21) equals **2261**. Notably, 2261 is a perfect multiple of 19.

The Perfectly Divisible Numbers

A number is considered perfectly divisible when it can be divided by another number without leaving a remainder. For example, when you divide 100 by 25, you get 4 without any remainder, so 100 is perfectly divisible by 25.

The Quran has six chapters (1, 2, 4, 5, 16, 30) where the total number of verses is perfectly divisible by the chapter number. The sum of their results (7 + 143 + 44 + 24 + 8 + 2) yields **228**, a number divisible by 19, further highlighting the remarkable mathematical coherence and precision within the Quran. *Refer to Table 7.4*

Verses ÷ Chapter No.

Example A

	V		C		V÷C
#1	7	÷	1	=	7
#2	286	÷	2	=	143
#3	176	÷	4	=	44
#4	120	÷	5	=	24
#5	128	÷	16	=	8
#6	60	÷	30	=	2
		TOTAL Σ			**228**

⇒ 228 ÷ **19**

Table 7.4

The sum of all chapter numbers, except for the first occurrence (2 + 4 + 5 + 16 + 30), equals 57, which is perfectly divisible by 19. Similarly, all verse numbers, except for the first occurrence, combined form a 14-digit long number 28617612012860 that is perfectly divisible by 19. The numbers in the last column of the verse numbers form the number 766080, which follows the rhythm of 19 being perfectly divisible by 19.

In the exploration of mathematical miracles, we uncover a remarkable fusion of Mathematics and the Quran. The presence of square numbers, cube numbers, perfectly divisible numbers, and the perch of the number 19 throughout the Quran's structure goes beyond mere coincidence. The answer to the crucial question of whether the Quran was compiled under divine guidance now seems to be clearer with the help of Mathematics.

8

THE MAGNIFICENT SEVEN

Unfazed by History, Mathematics keeps up its assault with a calculated and precise strike. Mathematics helps us probe into the 7 Mysterious Letters, the 7 Longest Chapters, the 7 Mystical Verses, the 7 Colors of Light, and the 7 Firmaments that form the theme - The Magnificent 7.

The number 7 itself is one of the numerical marvels in the Quran. The word "seven" (7) appears in 16 chapters, totalling 28 times in the Quran, which is a clear multiple of 7 (7 × 4). Its first occurrence is in Chapter 2, Verse 29, and its final occurrence is in Chapter 78, Verse 12. This means it is precisely spread across **77** chapters from Chapter 2 to 78, and 77 is also a distinct multiple of 7. This structured occurrence is not random but deliberate and methodical.

The first mention of 7 in the Quran, found in Chapter 2, Verse 29, reveals a mathematical signature. The difference between the digits of its verses (9 - 2) equals 7. Furthermore, the number 7 appears in exactly 16 chapters, and the sum of its digits (1 + 6) also equals 7, reaffirming its deliberate placement.

7 Mysterious Letters

In our continued quest to unravel the mathematical marvels of the Quran, let us explore the interesting world of palindromes.

A palindrome or a mirrored palindrome, as we know, is a word, number, or phrase that reads the same forwards and backward. "Radar," "madam," and 12321 are classic examples of a palindrome.

كل فى فلك

The phrase "كُلٌّ فِى فَلَكٍ", which translates to *"Everything is in rotation"*, comprising 7 letters **ك ل ف ى ف ل ك** and 3 words, reads the same both ways. The phrase appears twice in the Quran, precisely in Chapter 21:33 and Chapter 36:40.

The mathematical synchronization surrounding this mirrored palindrome is truly fascinating. When we multiply the chapter number by the verse number wherever it appears, we uncover an astonishing number. Multiplying 21 by 33 yields 693, and multiplying 36 by 40 yields 1440. Adding these results together (693 + 1440), we arrive at the astonishing number **2133**. This number 2133 remains constant, precisely matching the appended number of the first occurrence of the palindrome at Chapter 21:33. *(Refer to Table 8.1A)*

Palindrome

			C		V	Product
1st Time	A	كل فى فلك	**21**	:	**33**	(21 x 33) = 693
2nd Time	B	كل فى فلك	36	:	40	(36 x 40) = 1440
	SUM TOTAL =		(21 x 33) + (36 x 40)			**= 2133**

Table 8.1A

If 21 is excluded from the numbers, the remaining numbers form **333640**, which is perfectly divisible by 19. And if all the numbers are criss-crossed, the resulting number **21403633** is also divisible by 19.

Furthermore, the individual numbers 21 and 33 hold additional mathematical intrigue, being respectively the 12th and 21st composite numbers. Concatenating these numbers gives us "1221," another palindrome that reads the same forwards and backward. *(Refer to Table 8.1B).* Chapter 21 contains 112 verses. The combined number **21112** is also a palindrome.

Chapter No.	Verse No.
21	33
12TH *Composite No.*	21ST *Composite No.*
PALINDROME: **12:21**	

Table 8.1B

Are these intricacies mere coincidences, or do they hint at an intelligent design behind the compilation of the Quran? The presence of such sublime mathematics interwoven within its text certainly invites contemplation.

7 Longest Chapters

Yet another marvel of the Quran's compilation is its 7 longest Chapters, the chapters which have the highest number of verses. Consider the sum of the verses in these 7 longest chapters of the Quran: 286, 200, 176, 165, 206, 227, and 182, which equals **1442.**

Remarkably, Chapter 7 of the Quran has precisely 206 verses. Multiplying the Chapter number by its verses (7 x 206) also results in **1442.** Such precise calculations, where the sum of the 7 longest chapters matches the structure of the 7th chapter, highlight the melodious harmony that resonates within the Quran's composition and compilation. *Refer to Table 8.2 for details.*

÷ 19

3
2
7
6
7
6
4
3
2

7 Longest Chapters

	C		V	
#1	2	:	286	
#2	3	:	200	
#3	4	:	176	
#4	6	:	165	
#5	**7**	x	**206**	= **1442**
#6	26	:	227	
#7	37	:	182	
	TOTAL Σ =		**1442**	

÷ 19

8
0
7
6
0
2
8

Table 8.2

Remarkably, the chapter numbers presented in the ascending column create a sequence, **327676432**, which is divisible by 19. Similarly, the ascending middle column of the verse numbers forms another sequence, **8206708**, that is also perfectly divisible by 19. Furthermore, all the numbers in the verse column, only by moving the digit 1 to the start, form a synchronized sequence, **127656068206708221122**, which is divisible by 19. This means that the 30-digit number formed by combining all chapter and verse numbers from columns, **327676432127656068206708221122,** is perfectly divisible by 19:

These compelling examples of mathematical perfection reinforce the notion that the Quran's compilation exceeds human endeavor. The correlations between chapter numbers and the number of verses therein beckon us to contemplate the divine origin of this sacred text. Indeed, the Quran's flawless structure and numerical intricacies hint at a higher intelligence behind its composition and compilation.

❊ ❊ ❊

7 Mystical Verses

Let us now explore the mystical verses of *Surah Al-Fateha*, the opening chapter of the Quran. The name, *Al-Fateha* (**الفاتحة**), consists of 7 letters, and the chapter has 7 verses. However, before we unravel its mathematical mosaic, let us acknowledge the historical alterations that have affected the spellings of three of its words, namely *(Al-Aalamin)* ٱلْعَٰلَمِينَ [7 letters] vs. the original **الْعَالَمِينَ** [8 letters], and likewise, the word *(Seerat)* صِرَٰطَ [3 letters] vs. the original **صِرَاطَ** [4 letters], and the word *(Maalik)* مَٰلِكِ [3 letters] vs. the original **مَالِكِ** [4 letters]. We will discuss these *dagger-alif* alterations in a later chapter.

In our endeavor to reveal the original form of *Surah Al-Fateha*, we wield the arsenal of vowels, purging the introduced *dagger alifs* and restoring its pristine essence. *Refer to Table 8.3*

7 Mystical Verses				
CHAPTER 1 - AL-FATEHA الفاتحة		LINES	WORDS	LETTERS
بِسْمِ ٱللَّهِ ٱلرَّحْمَٰنِ ٱلرَّحِيمِ ۝		1	4	19
الْحَمْدُ لِلَّهِ رَبِّ الْعَالَمِينَ ۝		2	4	18
الرَّحْمَنِ الرَّحِيمِ ۝		3	2	12
مَالِكِ يَوْمِ الدِّينِ ۝		4	3	12
إِيَّاكَ نَعْبُدُ وَإِيَّاكَ نَسْتَعِينُ ۝		5	4	19
اِهْدِنَا الصِّرَاطَ الْمُسْتَقِيمَ ۝		6	3	19
صِرَاطَ الَّذِينَ أَنْعَمْتَ عَلَيْهِمْ		7	9	44
غَيْرِ الْمَغْضُوبِ عَلَيْهِمْ وَلَا الضَّالِّينَ ۝				
TOTAL Σ	1	7	29	143

Table 8.3: Al Fateha

Mathematically, *Surah Al-Fateha* can be described as Chapter 1 having 7 Verses and 29 Words. Appending these numbers 1,7, and 29, yields **1729**, a number replete with intriguing properties. 1729 can be described as a number divisible by 19; it stands as the product of two prime numbers, 19 and 91, where 91 is the mirror of 19. The sum of all its digits (1 + 7 + 2 + 9) equals 19, further emphasizing its mystical allure.

Hardy-Ramanujan Number

Moreover, 1729, known as the Hardy-Ramanujan number, holds a revered status in mathematics. 1729 is the smallest number that can be expressed as the sum of two cubes in two distinct ways. Mathematically, this is represented as:

$1729 = (1)^3 + (12)^3$	and	$1729 = (10)^3 + (9)^3$

Furthermore, 1729 unveils yet another layer of its mathematical splendor. It can be expressed as the difference between the squares of 55 and 36, as:

$1729 = (55)^2 - (36)^2$	and	$55 - 36 = \mathbf{19}$

Both the numbers 55 and 36 hold profound significance in the Quranic context. *Surah Rahman* (55) and *Surah Ya-Seen* (36) are both the Quran's key chapters. Intriguingly, the difference between 55 and 36 yields the number 19, further emphasizing the numerical harmony prevalent throughout the Quran.

CHAPTER NUMBERS of the 56 verses where the word RAHMAN appears							
1	1	2	13	17	19	19	19
19	19	19	19	19	19	19	19
19	19	19	19	19	20	20	20
20	21	21	21	21	25	25	25
25	26	27	36	36	36	36	41
43	43	43	43	43	43	43	50
55	59	67	67	67	67	78	78
SUM OF CHAPTER NUMBERS = 1729 = (19 x 91)							

Table 8.4

Moreover, the word *"Rahman"* (رحمٰن), which graces the opening line of the Holy Quran (1:1), also stands as a beacon of mathematics. In 56 verses, this illustrious word recurs 57 times across the Quranic text. 57 is a multiple of 19 (19 x 3). Astonishingly, the cumulative sum of all the chapter numbers wherein *"Rahman"* appears totals **1729**. *Refer to Table 8.4: Chapter Numbers where the word "Rahman" appears.*

As already mentioned, 1729 is the product of 19 x 91. Notably, the word *"Rahman"* also appears in Chapter 19, Verse 91, offering yet another glimpse into the numerical elegance embedded within the Quran's structure.

Quran **19:91**	أَن دَعَوۡاْ لِلرَّحۡمَٰنِ وَلَدٗا ۝
*(An da'aaw lil **Rahman** e walada)*	

Letters of Al-Fateha

But the numerical revelations do not cease there. *Surah Al-Fateha*, formed from 21 Arabic letters, harbours a plethora of mathematical intricacies. *Refer to Table 8.5*

- Of these 21 letters, 2 letters, ق and ذ stand unique, while 19 letters are repeated in the chapter. Appending the numbers of the unique and repeated letters yields **219**.
- Interestingly, of these unique letters, ق is the 21st letter of the Arabic Alphabet and ذ is the 9th letter, again leading to the number **219** when both positions are appended. The mirror number of 219 is 912, a multiple of 19.

Letters of Surah Fatiha		
2 Unique Letters	**19** Repeated Letters	Append = **219**
2 Unique Letters		
ق	ذ	
21st Letter	**9**th Letter	Append = **219**

Table 8.5

- Of the total 28 Arabic letters, *Surah Al-Fateha* consists of **21** letters, a multiple of 7. The 7 letters that are left out are all dotted letters :

ث- ج- خ- ز- ش- ظ- ف

- Out of the total 143 letters, the chapter consists of 38 (19 x 2) dotted letters, which are a multiple of 19, and the remaining 105 (7 x 35) letters without dots, which are in multiples of 7.
- Remarkably, the distribution of these 21 letters reflects a meticulous arrangement, with the first line containing **7** letters without dots, while the seventh line features **7** letters adorned with dots.
- Moreover, each of the 7 lines of *Surah Al-Fateha* ends with words ending in either the letters 'م' (M) or 'ن' (N). Across the chapter, there are 26 instances of both 'م' (M) and 'ن' (N). Excluding the 7-line endings, there are precisely 19 instances of these letters in the middle of the text, uncovering an intricate numerical pattern.

- Similarly, the letter أ (A) appears 26 times throughout Chapter 1. Remarkably, the final seventh line of the chapter contains 7 instances of the letter أ (A). Excluding this line, there are again **19** instances of the letter أ (A), reinforcing the chapter's mathematical precision and consistency.
- The significance of the first and last letters of the chapter, "ب" and "ن" respectively, further highlights its mathematical elegance. The repetition of "ن" 11 times and "ب" 4 times in the chapter leads to **114** upon appending, which is a multiple of 19, and also a number that aligns with the number of chapters (114) in the Quran.
- Additionally, the difference between these two numbers (11 – 4) is 7, once again highlighting and revealing the chapter's magnificent composition.

As we dive deep into the mathematical intricacies of *Surah Al-Fateha*, we are confronted with a profound question: Are these placements and connections merely coincidental, or do they hint at a deeper intelligence guiding the composition of the Quran? If mathematics is indeed the language of God, then the Quran, as the word of God, has indeed been adorned with mathematical beauty.

***

7 Colors of light.

The concept of seven colors, visible in a rainbow through the dispersion of white light, is a miraculous design found in nature. Scientifically, it is known that the light spectrum consists of exactly seven colors.

- The Quran, too, alludes to this connection in its mention of the word *"Alwaan"* أَلْوَانٌ (colors) exactly **7** times, spread across 4 different chapters. *Refer to Table 8.6*

7 Colors of Light

	C		V	TOTAL Σ	
#1	16	:	13	**114**	
#2	16	:	69		
#3	30	:	22	**114**	**49**
#4	35	:	27		
#5	2nd Time				
#6	35	:	28	**2128**	**49**
#7	39	:	21		
⇒	**171 : TOTAL**				
⇒	16303539 ÷ **19**				
⇒	162222 ÷ **19**				
⇒	2128 ÷ **19**				

Table 8.6

- The total of Chapter and Verse Numbers of the first 2 occurrences (16 + 13 + 16 + 69) equals **114**, a perfect multiple of 19.
- The total of Chapter and Verse Numbers of the next 2 occurrences (30 + 22 + 35 + 27) equals **114**, a perfect multiple of 19
- The total of the Verse Numbers of the 3rd and the 4th occurrence (22+27) equals **49**, the square of number 7.
- The total of the Verse Numbers of the 6th and the 7th occurrence (28+21) also equals **49**, the square of the number 7.
- The Verse Numbers of the 7th and the 6th occurrence form **2128**, a number divisible by both 7 and 19, while the number 76 is also apparent from the Verse Numbers, again perfectly divisible by 19.
- Furthermore, the sum of the chapter numbers where *"Alwaan"* appears (16 + 16 + 30 + 35 + 35 + 39) equals **171**, which is a perfect multiple of the number 19.

- What's more astonishing is that the appended number formed from the 4-chapter number sequence **16303539** is also divisible by 19.
- The digits appearing in the first column of all six verses, where *"Alwaan"* is mentioned, form the number **162222,** which is divisible by 19, adding layers of mathematical precision to the Quran's structure.

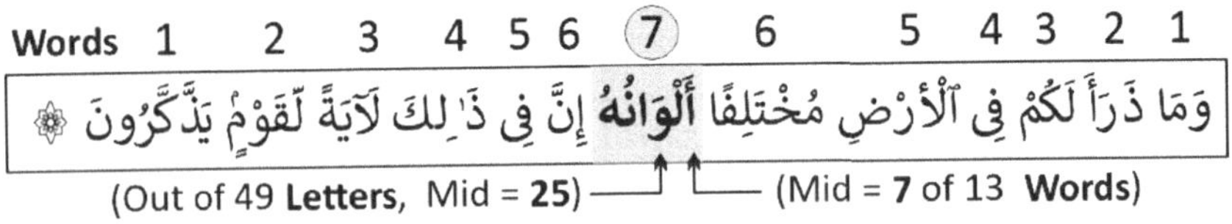

Table 8.7: *Chapter 16:13*

- The first appearance of the word *"Alwaan"* **أَلْوَانُ** (colors) is in Chapter 16, Verse 13, consisting of 13 words. *Refer to Table 8.7*
- Strikingly, the 7th word in this verse is colors, *"Alwaan,"* placed at the exact center, emphasizing its significance.
- This verse contains 49 letters, the square of 7, further showcasing mathematical symmetry.
- The center letter of the verse, the 25th letter, is **ن** ("Noon"), which is the 27th letter in the Arabic Alphabet. Appending both the numbers, we get **2527**, which is divisible by 19.
- The last word in the line, **يَذَّكَّرُونَ** *"yazzakkarun"*, appears as a verse ending in the entire Quran, exactly 7 times, once again maintaining the mathematical balance. Its 1st appearance is in 6:126 and its 7th appearance is in 37:13. The difference between (6126 – 3713) is **2413**, which is perfectly divisible by 19.

* * *

7 Firmaments

The Quran differentiates the sky *"Samaa"* from the firmaments *"Samawaat"*, suggesting that they are distinct but interconnected elements of creation. The sky refers to the visible expanse we see when we look up from Earth. The firmament is a vast, protective dome stretched over the Earth. It is envisioned as a solid, curved, layered structure beyond the sky, functioning as a containment boundary.

Many ancient cultures, immersed in higher philosophical knowledge and the understanding of ultimate reality, believed in the existence of the firmament and that it has 7 distinct curved layers that form a dome above the sky. They understood that the firmament acted as a lens, which was the reason for light to bend, form an arc, and create phenomena like rainbows. They also believed the echoes of thunder were caused by sound waves bouncing off the solid dome. They considered that the firmament was the reason for the earth's atmospheric pressure and was responsible for regulating wind patterns, storms, and weather changes. What is known today as the Van Allen Belts, which is a barrier, an impenetrable boundary preventing direct passage beyond Earth, according to them, was the firmament.

The Mathematics of the 7 Firmaments

The Quran refers to these celestial multiple layers as *"Saba samawaat"* (seven firmaments) or *"As-samawaat as-saba"* (the seven firmaments). Mathematics, once again, steps forward as a guide to unravel the digital encoding in the Quran. The Quran refers to the **7** firmaments exactly 7 times across 7 different chapters. This is no mere coincidence; it is an embedded design of the Quran. *Refer to Table 8.8*

7 Firmaments			
	C		V
#1	2	:	29
#2	17	:	44
#3	23	:	86
#4	41	:	12
#5	65	:	12
#6	67	:	3
#7	71	:	15
TOTAL	**286**		**201**

Table 8.8

- Appending the chapter numbers 2, 17, 23, 41, 65, 67, and 71, where the references occur, we get the number **2172341656771**, which is perfectly divisible by 19.
- Appending the verse numbers (29, 44, 86, 12, 12, 3, and 15) of these references, we get **2944861212315**, which is also perfectly divisible by 19 - the mathematical signature of the Quran.
- Furthermore, the sum of all the chapter and verse numbers (286 + 201) gives us **487**, where the sum of its digits (4 + 8 + 7) equals 19, reaffirming the Quran's intricate numerical design.

This alignment of scientific facts with mathematical harmony in the Quran is more than coincidental; it illustrates an intricately flawless design and intentional compilation. The scientific principles of nature are presented with mathematical exactitude, reinforcing the Quran's message through knowledge, wisdom, and precision.

9

THE SYMMETRY OF WORDS

History, though valiant, it begins to falter under the weight of mathematical patterns and symmetries. Our relentless pursuit of demonstrating the divine compilation of the Quran unveils yet another layer of its miraculous structure: the symmetry of words. Within the Quranic text, certain verses serve as central points for two or more words. These verses exhibit a remarkable symmetry and balance with respect to their position. Let us examine several examples to understand and eliminate any possibility of coincidence and provide clear evidence about the symmetry of words in the existing compilation of the Quran.

The Center Verse 9:71 - Example #1

WORD / PHRASE	No. of Times	Half / Mid	Mid Verse
As-Salaat الصَّلٰوةَ	64	32	**9:71**
Az-Zakaat الزَّكٰوةَ	28	14	**9:71**
Salaat + Zakaat الصَّلٰوةَ + الزَّكٰوةَ	26	13	**9:71**

Consider the words *"As-Salaat"* (prayer) and *"Az-Zakaat"* (charity). The word *"As-Salaat"* appears 64 times in the Quran, with Verse **9:71** serving as its central point at the 32nd position. This means that from the beginning of the Quran until 9:71, the word *"As-Salaat"* appears 32 times, and after 9:71, it appears 32 times again.

Similarly, *"Az-Zakaat"* appears 28 times, also with Verse 9:71 as its midpoint at the 14th position. This indicates that the word *"Az-Zakaat"* appears 14 times in the Quran from the beginning until 9:71, and then appears 14 times again after 9:71.

Where both words *"As-Salaat + Az-Zakaat"* appear together in a verse, Verse 9:71 remains their central point, with an equal distribution before and after it. *"As-Salaat + Az-Zakaat"* appear together in 26 verses. So, from the beginning of the Quran until 9:71, the words *"As-Salaat + Az-Zakaat"* appear together 13 times, and after 9:71, they appear together 13 times as well.

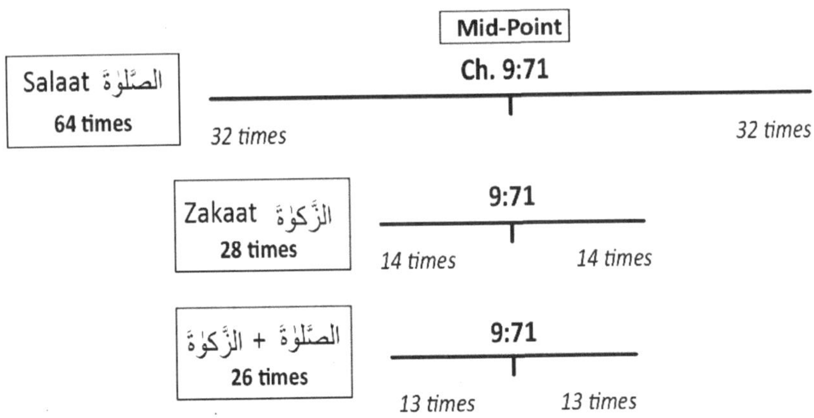

The compilation of the Quran is so perfect that the words *"Salaat"*, *"Zakaat"* and combined *"Salaat + Zakaat"*, all appear an equal number of times before and after Verse 9:71

Refer to Table 9.1 showing all the occurrences of **الصَّلٰوةَ** *(As-Salaat)*, **الزَّكٰوةَ** *(Az-Zakaat)*, and *"As-Salaat + Az-Zakaat"* **الصَّلٰوةَ + الزَّكٰوةَ** in the Quran.

* * *

The Center Verse 27:1 - Example #2

WORD / PHRASE	No. of Times	Half / Mid	Mid Verse
Al-Quran القرآن	50	25	**27:1**
Quran قرآن	68	34	**27:1**

Another intriguing example involves the words *"Al-Quran"* and *"Quran"*, which are both considered separate words. The word *"Al-Quran"* appears 50 times in the Quran, with Verse **27:1** as its center at the 25th position. This means that from the beginning of the Quran until verse 27:1, the word *"Al-Quran"* appears 25 times. Similarly, after verse 27:1, the word *"Al-Quran"* appears another 25 times.

Likewise, *"Quran"* appears 68 times, again with Verse 27:1 as its midpoint at the 34th position. The word *"Quran"* is a subset of the word *"Al-Quran"*, so it is also counted whenever the word *"Al-Quran"* appears. This means that from the beginning of the Quran until verse 27:1, the word *"Quran"* occurs 34 times. After verse 27:1, the word *"Quran"* also appears another 34 times.

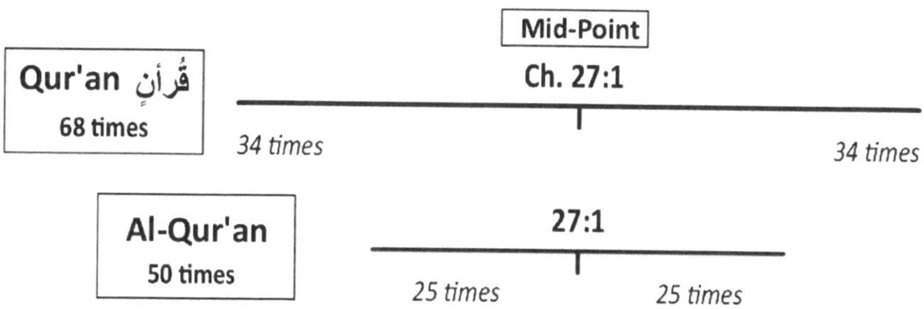

The compilation of the Quran is so remarkable that the words *"Al-Quran"* and *"Quran"* appear an equal number of times before and after Verse 27:1. This symmetry demonstrates a deliberate balance in the distribution of these words throughout the Quranic text.

Refer to Table 9.2 showing the frequency of the word *"Al-Quran"* **القُرانِ** and *"Quran"* **قُرانٍ** in the Quran.

Completeness of the Quran

Additionally, the numerical relationship within the occurrences of *"Al-Quran"* holds further significance. The first occurrence of *"Al-Quran"* is in Chapter 2:185, while the last is in Chapter 84:21. When perceived as a complete number, the difference between these numbers (8421 – 2185) equals **6236**, which is also the total number of verses in the Quran, that is, 6236.

8421 – 2185 = 6236

How could the completeness of the Quran be stated more eloquently, showing the difference between the first and last occurrences of the word *"Al-Quran,"* and revealing the total number of verses in the Quran?

Two Letters and Two Chapters

Two Letters **ق** and **ن** also form two unique *Muqattaat* (Mysterious Letters) which start Chapters 50 and 68, respectively.

- The word *"Quran"* **قُرانٍ** in Arabic begins with the letter "**ق**" and ends with the letter "**ن**". Chapter 50 begins with the letter "**ق**" and on the other hand, Chapter 68 begins and ends with the letter "**ن**". Both identical words *"Al-Quran"* **القُرانِ** and *"Quran"* **قُرانٍ** appear 50 times and 68 times respectively in the Quran.
- The Quran contains only three chapters that start with the letter "**ق**" and end with the letter "**ن**". These chapters are numbered 23, 58, and 109. The total (23 + 58 + 109) of these chapter numbers is **190**, which is a perfect multiple of 19.
- Remarkably, from Chapters 50 to 68, there are exactly **19** chapters.

* * *

All Occurences of

Zakaat
الزَّكوٰة

#	C	:	V
#1	2	:	43
#2	2	:	83
#3	2	:	110
#4	2	:	177
#5	2	:	277
#6	4	:	77
#7	4	:	162
#8	5	:	12
#9	5	:	55
#10	7	:	156
#11	9	:	5
#12	9	:	11
#13	9	:	18
#14	9	:	71
#15	19	:	31
#16	19	:	55
#17	21	:	73
#18	22	:	41
#19	22	:	78
#20	24	:	37
#21	24	:	56
#22	27	:	3
#23	31	:	4
#24	33	:	33
#25	41	:	7
#26	58	:	13
#27	73	:	20
#28	98	:	5

Salaat
الصَّلوٰة

#	C	:	V
#1	2	:	3
#2	2	:	43
#3	2	:	45
#4	2	:	83
#5	2	:	110
#6	2	:	153
#7	2	:	177
#8	2	:	238
#9	2	:	277
#10	4	:	43
#11	4	:	77
#12	4	:	101
#13	4	:	102
#14	4	:	103
#15	2nd time		
#16	3rd time		
#17	4	:	142
#18	4	:	162
#19	5	:	6
#20	5	:	12
#21	5	:	55
#22	5	:	58
#23	5	:	91
#24	5	:	106
#25	6	:	72
#26	7	:	170
#27	8	:	3
#28	9	:	5
#29	9	:	11
#30	9	:	18
#31	9	:	54
#32	9	:	71
#33	10	:	87
#34	11	:	114
#35	13	:	22
#36	14	:	31
#37	14	:	37
#38	14	:	40
#39	17	:	78
#40	19	:	31
#41	19	:	55
#42	19	:	59
#43	20	:	14
#44	20	:	132
#45	21	:	73
#46	22	:	35
#47	22	:	41
#48	22	:	78
#49	24	:	37
#50	24	:	56
#51	27	:	3
#52	29	:	45
#53	2nd time		
#54	30	:	31
#55	31	:	4
#56	31	:	17
#57	33	:	33
#58	35	:	18
#59	35	:	29
#60	42	:	38
#61	58	:	13
#62	62	:	10
#63	73	:	20
#64	98	:	5

الصَّلوٰة + الزَّكوٰة

#	C	:	V
#1	2	:	43
#2	2	:	83
#3	2	:	110
#4	2	:	177
#5	2	:	277
#6	4	:	77
#7	4	:	162
#8	5	:	12
#9	5	:	55
#10	9	:	5
#11	9	:	11
#12	9	:	18
#13	9	:	71
#14	19	:	31
#15	19	:	55
#16	21	:	73
#17	22	:	41
#18	22	:	78
#19	24	:	37
#20	24	:	56
#21	27	:	3
#22	31	:	4
#23	33	:	33
#24	58	:	13
#25	73	:	20
#26	98	:	5

Table 9.1: All occurrences in the Quran

All Occurences of

Qur'an
قُرأنٍ

#	C	V	#	C	V
#1	2	185	#35	27	6
#2	4	82	#36	27	76
#3	5	101	#37	27	92
#4	6	19	#38	28	85
#5	7	204	#39	30	58
#6	9	111	#40	34	31
#7	10	15	#41	36	2
#8	10	37	#42	36	69
#9	10	61	#43	38	1
#10	12	2	#44	39	28
#11	12	3	#45	39	27
#12	13	31	#46	41	3
#13	15	1	#47	41	26
#14	15	87	#48	41	44
#15	15	91	#49	42	7
#16	16	98	#50	43	3
#17	17	9	#51	43	31
#18	17	41	#52	46	29
#19	17	45	#53	47	24
#20	17	46	#54	50	1
#21	17	60	#55	50	45
#22	17	78	#56	54	17
#23	2nd time		#57	54	22
#24	17	82	#58	54	32
#25	17	88	#59	54	40
#26	17	89	#60	55	2
#27	17	106	#61	56	77
#28	18	54	#62	59	21
#29	20	2	#63	72	1
#30	20	113	#64	73	4
#31	20	114	#65	73	20
#32	25	30	#66	76	23
#33	25	32	#67	84	21
#34	**27**	**1**	**#68**	85	21

Al-Qur'an
القُرأنٍ

#	C	V	#	C	V
#1	2	185	#26	27	6
#2	4	82	#27	27	76
#3	5	101	#28	27	92
#4	6	19	#29	28	85
#5	7	204	#30	30	58
#6	9	111	#31	34	31
#7	10	37	#32	36	2
#8	12	3	#33	38	1
#9	15	87	#34	39	27
#10	15	91	#35	41	26
#11	16	98	#36	43	31
#12	17	9	#37	46	29
#13	17	41	#38	47	24
#14	17	45	#39	50	1
#15	17	46	#40	50	45
#16	17	60	#41	54	17
#17	17	82	#42	54	22
#18	17	88	#43	54	32
#19	17	89	#44	54	40
#20	18	54	#45	55	2
#21	20	2	#46	59	21
#22	20	114	#47	73	4
#23	25	30	#48	73	20
#24	25	32	#49	76	23
#25	**27**	**1**	**#50**	84	21

Table 9.2: All occurrences in the Quran

The Center Verse 20:19 - Example #3

WORD / PHRASE	No. of Times	Half / Mid	Mid Verse
Musa موسىٰ	100	50	**20:19**
Ya Musa يٰموسىٰ	24	12	**20:19**
Musa with Others موسىٰ هٰمٰنَ قٰرونَ هٰرونَ فرعون	136	68	**20:19**

In the Quran, 100 specific verses only mention the name *"Musa"* موسىٰ (Moses) and do not include any other name in the same verse.

Then, there are a total of 136 verses in the Quran which include the exclusive verses with the name *"Musa"* موسىٰ and verses with the name *"Musa"* along with other names such as *Firaun, Haroon, Qaroon*, and *Hamaan* (هٰمٰنَ قٰرونَ هٰرونَ فرعون) in the same verse.

The exclusive verses having only the name *"Musa"* and the phrase *"Ya Musa"* (O Moses) exhibit similar symmetry. *"Musa"* appears 100 times, with Verse **20:19** as its midpoint, while *"Ya Musa"* appears 24 times and Verse 20:19 similarly remains its center. This means that from the start of the Quran till 20:19, the name *"Musa"* appears 50 times, and *"Ya Musa"* appears 12 times. Similarly, after verse 20:19, the word *"Musa"* appears another 50 times, and *"Ya Musa"* appears 12 times.

Furthermore, for all 136 occurrences of *"Musa"* alongside other names like *Firaun, Haroon, Qaroon,* and *Hamaan* (هٰمٰنَ قٰرونَ هٰرونَ فرعون), Verse 20:19 remains the central point. This means that from the start of the Quran till 20:19, all occurrences of the name *"Musa"* appear 68 times. Similarly, after verse 20:19, the name *"Musa"* appears another 68 times.

Tables 9.3a, 9.3b, and 9.3c show the entire occurrences of *"Musa"*, *"Ya Musa"*, and all occurrences of *"Musa"* (along with other names such as *Firaun, Haroon, Qaroon, and Hamaan*), respectively.

All Occurences of

Musa (Moses) موسیٰ — **Musa** *(Continued...)* موسیٰ

#	C	V	#	C	V	#	C	V	#	C	V
#1	2	51	#35	2nd time		#69	20	36	#103	28	19
#2	2	53	#36	7	143	#70	20	40	#104	28	20
#3	2	54	#37	2nd time		#71	20	49	#105	28	29
#4	2	55	#38	7	144	#72	20	57	#106	28	30
#5	2	60	#39	7	148	#73	20	61	#107	28	31
#6	2	61	#40	7	150	#74	20	65	#108	28	36
#7	2	67	#41	7	154	#75	20	67	#109	28	37
#8	2	87	#42	7	155	#76	20	70	#110	28	38
#9	2	92	#43	7	159	#77	20	77	#111	28	43
#10	2	108	#44	7	160	#78	20	83	#112	28	44
#11	2	136	#45	10	75	#79	20	86	#113	28	48
#12	2	246	#46	10	77	#80	20	88	#114	2nd time	
#13	2	248	#47	10	80	#81	20	91	#115	28	76
#14	3	84	#48	10	81	#82	21	48	#116	29	39
#15	4	153	#49	10	83	#83	22	44	#117	32	23
#16	2nd time		#50	10	84	#84	23	45	#118	33	7
#17	4	164	#51	10	87	#85	23	49	#119	33	69
#18	5	20	#52	10	88	#86	25	35	#120	37	114
#19	5	22	#53	11	17	#87	26	10	#121	37	120
#20	5	24	#54	11	96	#88	26	43	#122	40	23
#21	6	84	#55	11	110	#89	26	45	#123	40	26
#22	6	91	#56	14	5	#90	26	48	#124	40	27
#23	6	154	#57	14	6	#91	26	52	#125	40	37
#24	7	103	#58	14	8	#92	26	61	#126	40	53
#25	7	104	#59	17	2	#93	26	63	#127	41	45
#26	7	115	#60	17	101	#94	26	65	#128	42	13
#27	7	117	#61	2nd time		#95	26	7	#129	43	46
#28	7	122	#62	18	60	#96	27	9	#130	46	12
#29	7	127	#63	18	66	#97	27	10	#131	46	30
#30	7	128	#64	19	51	#98	28	3	#132	51	38
#31	7	131	#65	20	9	#99	28	7	#133	53	36
#32	7	134	#66	20	11	#100	28	10	#134	61	5
#33	7	138	#67	20	17	#101	28	15	#135	79	15
#34	7	142	**#68**	**20**	**19**	#102	28	18	**#136**	87	19

Table 9.3a: All occurrences in the Quran

All Occurences of

Only Musa موسىٰ | **Only Musa** *(...Continued)* موسىٰ

	C		V		C		V		C		V		C		V
#1	2	:	51	#26	7	:	148	#51	20	:	36	#76	28	:	7
#2	2	:	53	#27	7	:	150	#52	20	:	40	#77	28	:	10
#3	2	:	54	#28	7	:	154	#53	20	:	49	#78	28	:	15
#4	2	:	55	#29	7	:	155	#54	20	:	57	#79	28	:	18
#5	2	:	60	#30	7	:	159	#55	20	:	61	#80	28	:	19
#6	2	:	61	#31	7	:	160	#56	20		65	#81	28	:	20
#7	2	:	67	#32	10	:	77	#57	20	:	67	#82	28	:	29
#8	2	:	92	#33	10	:	80	#58	20	:	77	#83	28	:	30
#9	2	:	108	#34	10	:	81	#59	20	:	83	#84	28	:	31
#10	2	:	246	#35	10	:	84	#60	20	:	86	#85	28	:	36
#11	4	:	153	#36	10	:	87	#61	20	:	88	#86	28	:	37
#12	4	:	164	#37	10	:	88	#62	20	:	91	#87	28	:	43
#13	5	:	20	#38	11	:	17	#63	22	:	44	#88	28	:	44
#14	5	:	22	#39	11	:	96	#64	23	:	49	#89	28	:	48
#15	5	:	24	#40	11	:	110	#65	25	:	35	#90	32	:	23
#16	6	:	91	#41	14	:	5	#66	26	:	10	#91	33	:	69
#17	6	:	154	#42	14	:	8	#67	26	:	43	#92	40	:	23
#18	7	:	115	#43	17	:	2	#68	26	:	45	#93	40	:	27
#19	7	:	117	#44	18	:	60	#69	26	:	52	#94	40	:	53
#20	7	:	128	#45	18	:	66	#70	26	:	61	#95	41	:	45
#21	7	:	131	#46	19	:	51	#71	26	:	63	#96	46	:	12
#22	7	:	134	#47	20	:	9	#72	26	:	65	#97	46	:	30
#23	7	:	138	#48	20	:	11	#73	26	:	7	#98	53	:	36
#24	7	:	143	#49	20	:	17	#74	27	:	9	#99	61	:	5
#25	7	:	144	**#50**	**20**	**:**	**19**	#75	27	:	10	**#100**	79	:	15

Ya Musa يٰموسىٰ | **Ya Musa** يٰموسىٰ

	C		V		C		V		C		V		C		V
#1	2	:	55	#7	7	:	138	#13	20	:	36	#19	27	:	9
#2	2	:	61	#8	7	:	144	#14	20	:	40	#20	27	:	10
#3	5	:	22	#9	17	:	101	#15	20	:	49	#21	28	:	19
#4	5	:	24	#10	20	:	11	#16	20	:	57	#22	28	:	20
#5	7	:	115	#11	20	:	17	#17	20		65	#23	28	:	30
#6	7	:	134	**#12**	**20**	**:**	**19**	#18	20	:	83	**#24**	28	:	31

Table 9.3b and Table 9.3c: All occurrences in the Quran

The Center Verse 26:44 - Example #4

WORD / PHRASE	No. of Times	Half / Mid	Mid Verse
(Firaun [Pharaoh]) فرعون	38	19	**26:44**
(Firaun) with Others فرعون هٰمٰنَ قٰرونَ هٰرونَ موسىٰ	67	34	**26:44**

In the Quran, 38 precise verses only mention the name *"Firaun"* [Pharaoh] فرعون exclusively and do not include any other name in the same verse.

Then, there are 67 verses in the Quran where the name *"Firaun"* فرعون is mentioned along with other names such as *Musa, Haroon, Qaroon,* and *Hamaan* (موسىٰ هٰرونَ قٰرونَ هٰمٰنَ) in the same verse.

In the Quran, the name *"Firaun"* [Pharaoh] appears in 38 verses, and Verse **26:44** enacts as the midpoint. This means that from the start of the Quran till 26:44, the name *"Firaun"* appears in 19 verses. Similarly, after verse 26:44, the word *"Firaun"* appears in another 19 verses.

Furthermore, for all 67 verses with *"Firaun"* alongside other names like *Musa, Haroon, Qaroon,* and *Hamaan* (موسىٰ هٰرونَ قٰرونَ هٰمٰنَ), Verse 26:44 remains the central point. This means that from the start of the Quran till 26:44, all occurrences of the name *"Firaun"* appear in 33 verses. Similarly, after verse 26:44, the name *"Firaun"* appears in another 33 verses.

Table 9.4a shows the verses with occurrences of only "*Firaun*" and *Table 9.4b* shows verses with the name "*Firaun*" (along with other names such as *Musa, Haroon, Qaroon,* and *Hamaan*).

This example, along with others, highlights the presence of symmetrical patterns and harmony within the text of the Quran.

All Occurences of

Only Firaun (Pharaoh) فرعون

#	C		V	#	C		V
#1	7	:	109	#20	26	:	53
#2	7	:	113	#21	27	:	12
#3	7	:	123	#22	28	:	4
#4	7	:	137	#23	28	:	9
#5	10	:	79	#24	28	:	32
#6	10	:	90	#25	38	:	12
#7	11	:	97	#26	40	:	29
#8	17	:	102	#27	40	:	45
#9	20	:	24	#28	43	:	51
#10	20	:	43	#29	44	:	17
#11	20	:	60	#30	44	:	31
#12	20	:	78	#31	50	:	13
#13	20	:	79	#32	66	:	11
#14	23	:	46	#33	69	:	9
#15	26	:	11	#34	73	:	15
#16	26	:	16	#35	73	:	16
#17	26	:	23	#36	79	:	17
#18	26	:	41	#37	85	:	18
#19	**26**	**:**	**44**	**#38**	89	:	10

Firaun + Others فرعون

#	C		V	#	C		V
#1	2	:	49	#35	26	:	53
#2	2	:	50	#36	27	:	12
#3	3	:	11	#37	28	:	3
#4	7	:	103	#38	28	:	4
#5	7	:	104	#39	28	:	6
#6	7	:	109	#40	28	:	8
#7	7	:	113	#41	28	:	9
#8	7	:	123	#42	28	:	32
#9	7	:	127	#43	28	:	38
#10	7	:	130	#44	29	:	39
#11	7	:	137	#45	38	:	12
#12	7	:	141	#46	40	:	24
#13	8	:	52	#47	40	:	26
#14	8	:	54	#48	40	:	28
#15	10	:	75	#49	40	:	29
#16	10	:	79	#50	40	:	36
#17	10	:	83	#51	40	:	37
#18	10	:	88	#52	40	:	45
#19	10	:	90	#53	40	:	46
#20	11	:	97	#54	43	:	46
#21	14	:	6	#55	43	:	51
#22	17	:	101	#56	44	:	17
#23	17	:	102	#57	44	:	31
#24	20	:	24	#58	50	:	13
#25	20	:	43	#59	51	:	38
#26	20	:	60	#60	54	:	41
#27	20	:	78	#61	66	:	11
#28	20	:	79	#62	69	:	9
#29	23	:	46	#63	73	:	15
#30	26	:	11	#64	73	:	16
#31	26	:	16	#65	79	:	17
#32	26	:	23	#66	85	:	18
#33	26	:	41	**#67**	89	:	10
#34	**26**	**:**	**44**				

Table 9.4a - All occurrences in the Quran - Table 9.4b

The Center Verse 5:78 - Example #5

WORD / PHRASE			Half / Mid	Mid Verse
Esa عيسَى	No. Of Times	25	13	**5:78**
Maryam مَريَم	No. Of Verses	31	16	**5:78**

The names *"Esa"*(Jesus) and *"Maryam"* (Mary) also exhibit symmetry in their occurrences. The name *"Esa"* appears 25 times, with Verse **5:78** as its midpoint, while the name *"Maryam"* appears in 31 verses, again with Verse 5:78 as its center. This means that from the start of the Quran till 5:78, the name *"Esa"* appears 12 times, and verses with the name *"Maryam"* appear 15 times. Similarly, after verse 5:78, the name *"Esa"* appears another 12 times, and verses with the name *"Maryam"* appear another 15 times.

The 19th time *"Esa"* is mentioned in the Quran is in the 19th Chapter. The last mention of *"Maryam"* in the Quran appears in Chapter 66, verse 12. The appended number **6612** is perfectly divisible by 19, and its mirror, 2166, is also a perfect multiple of 19, given as (19 x 114).

This balance underscores the interconnectedness of these figures within the Quranic narrative, such that the name *"Esa"* and verses with the name of his mother *"Maryam"* appear an equal number of times before and after Verse 5:78

Table 9.5 shows all the occurrences of *"Esa"* **عيسَى** and all verses with the name *"Maryam"* **مَريَم**

The journey into the intricate symmetries of the Quran continues, each revelation unveiling layers of divine craftsmanship that defy human comprehension. As we search deeper into the text, the evidence of its divine compilation becomes increasingly apparent, challenging all the conventional narratives.

All Occurences of

Esa (Jesus) عيسَى

#	C		V	#	C		V
#1	2	:	87	#14	5	:	110
#2	2	:	136	#15	5	:	112
#3	2	:	253	#16	5	:	114
#4	3	:	45	#17	5	:	116
#5	3	:	52	#18	6	:	85
#6	3	:	55	**#19**	19	:	34
#7	3	:	59	#20	33	:	7
#8	3	:	84	#21	42	:	13
#9	4	:	157	#22	43	:	63
#10	4	:	163	#23	57	:	27
#11	4	:	171	#24	61	:	6
#12	5	:	46	**#25**	61	:	14
#13	**5**	**:**	**78**				

Maryam مَريَم

#	C		V	#	C		V
#1	2	:	87	#17	5	:	110
#2	2	:	253	#18	5	:	112
#3	3	:	36	#19	5	:	114
#4	3	:	37	#20	5	:	116
#5	3	:	42	#21	9	:	31
#6	3	:	43	#22	19	:	16
#7	3	:	44	#23	19	:	27
#8	3	:	45	#24	19	:	34
#9	4	:	156	#25	23	:	50
#10	4	:	157	#26	33	:	7
#11	4	:	171	#27	43	:	57
#12	5	:	17	#28	57	:	27
#13	5	:	46	#29	61	:	6
#14	5	:	72	#30	61	:	14
#15	5	:	75	**#31**	66	:	12
#16	**5**	**:**	**78**				

Table 9.5: All occurrences in the Quran

* * *

The Center Verse 5:110 - Example #6

WORD / PHRASE	No. of Times	Half / Mid	Mid Verse
Esa Ibn-e-Maryam عيسَى ابنِ مَريَم	16	8	**5:110**
Ibn-e-Maryam ابنِ مَريَم	23	12	**5:110**

The full name *"Esa Ibn-e-Maryam"* (Jesus, son of Mary) and the title *"Ibn-e-Maryam"* (son of Mary) are used in the Quran to refer to Esa (Jesus). The name *"Esa Ibn-e-Maryam"* appears 16 times in the Quran, and Verse **5:110** is the midpoint of its occurrences. Before and after this verse, the name appears an equal number of times.

Intriguingly, the shorter form *"Ibn-e-Maryam"* appears 23 times, with Verse 5:110 remaining the central point. This means that from the start of the Quran till 5:110, the name *"Esa Ibn-e-Maryam"* appears 8 times, and "Ibn-e-Maryam" appears 11 times. Similarly, after verse 5:110, the name *"Esa Ibn-e-Maryam"* appears another 8 times, and *"Ibn-e-Maryam"* appears another 11 times, emphasizing a meticulous balance in its distribution. Again, this highlights the precision in the Quran's composition, ensuring symmetry in the usage of these names.

All Occurences of											
Esa Ibn Maryam عيسَى ابنَ مَريَمَ						Ibn Maryam ابنَ مَريَمَ					
	C	V		C	V		C	V		C	V
#1	2	87	#9	5	112	#1	2	87	#13	5	112
#2	2	253	#10	5	114	#2	2	253	#14	5	114
#3	3	45	#11	5	116	#3	3	45	#15	5	116
#4	4	157	#12	19	34	#4	4	157	#16	9	31
#5	4	171	#13	33	7	#5	4	171	#17	19	34
#6	5	46	#14	57	27	#6	5	17	#18	23	50
#7	5	78	#15	61	6	#7	2nd time		#19	33	7
#8	**5**	**110**	**#16**	61	14	#8	5	46	#20	43	57
						#9	5	72	#21	57	27
						#10	5	75	#22	61	6
						#11	5	78	**#23**	61	14
						#12	**5**	**110**			

Table 9.6: All occurrences in the Quran

In exploring the Quran's profound symmetries, we uncover yet another layer of numerical precision in the names *"Esa"*, *"Ibn-e-Maryam"* and *"Maryam"*, revealing an amazing harmony.

- The name *"Esa"* appears in 11 chapters of the Quran, specifically (2, 3, 4, 5, 6, **19**, 33, 42, 43, 57, 61). Remarkably, the center chapter among these is Chapter **19** *(Maryam)*, serving as a focal point for the distribution of this significant name.
- Exploring deeper and examining the title *"Ibn-e-Maryam"* (Son of Mary), the title is mentioned in 11 Chapters (2, 3, 4, 5, 9, **19**, 23, 33, 43, 57, 61) of the Quran. Once again, the center chapter remains consistent at Chapter **19**.
- The name *"Maryam"* is mentioned in 12 chapters of the Quran, specifically (2, 3, 4, 5, 9, **19**, 23, 33, 43, 57, 61, 66). The center chapter maintains its position at Chapter **19**, highlighting the numerical symmetry that permeates the Quran.

* * *

The Center Verse 24:35 - Example #7

WORD / PHRASE	No. of Times	Half / Mid	Mid Verse
Nur نّور	8	4	**24:35**
Nur with other variations نّور بِنورِ النّورِ وَنورٌ نورُهُم	46	23	**24:35**

Researching the word *"Nur"* (light) in the Quran. It appears 8 times, with Verse **24:35**, known as *Ayat-e-Nur*, marking its midpoint at the phrase :

نُّورٌ عَلَىٰ نُورٍ	"Nur-un ala Nur *(Light upon Light)*

From the start of the Quran till 24:35, only the word *"Nur"* (light) exclusively appears 4 times. Similarly, after verse 24:35, the word *"Nur"* appears another 4 times.

From the start of the Quran till 24:35, the word *"Nur" and its variations,* appear 23 times. After verse 24:35, the word *"Nur" and its variations,* appear another 23 times, totalling 46 times.

Both the exclusive word *"Nur"* and also Nur with its variations, with its prefixes and suffixes (بِنورِ النّورِ وَنورٌ نورُهُم) maintain a meticulous balance before and after this verse 24:35. *Table 9.7A and 9.7B* shows all the occurrences of *"Nur"* نّورِ and Nur with all its variations.

All Occurences of

Nur (Light) نُورٌ

	C	V		C	V		C	V		C	V
#1	5	15	#3	24	35	#5	3rd time		#7	39	22
#2	9	32	**#4**	**24**	**35**	#6	24	40	**#8**	61	8
				(2nd time)						*TOTAL*	*152*

All Variations of Nur نُورٌ

	C	V		C	V		C	V		C	V
#1	2	17	#12	7	157	#24	3rd time		#35	57	12
#2	2	257	#13	9	32	#25	4th time		#36	57	13
#3	2nd time		#14	2nd time		#26	5th time		#37	2nd time	
#4	4	174	#15	10	5	#27	24	40	#38	57	19
#5	5	15	#16	11	40	#28	2nd time		#39	57	28
#6	5	16	#17	13	16	#29	33	43	#40	61	8
#7	5	44	#18	14	1	#30	35	20	#41	2nd time	
#8	5	46	#19	14	5	#31	39	22	#42	64	8
#9	6	1	#20	19	63	#32	39	69	#43	65	11
#10	6	91	#21	23	27	#33	42	52	#44	66	8
#11	6	122	#22	24	35	#34	57	9	#45	2nd time	
			#23	**24**	**35**				**#46**	71	16
				(2nd time)							

Table 9.7A and 9.7B: All occurrences in the Quran

The Center Verse 37:74 - Example #8

WORD / PHRASE	No. of Times	Half / Mid	Mid Verse
Mukhlis مُخلَص	20	10	**37:74**
Mukhliseen مُخلَصِينَ	15	8	**37:74**
Al-Mukhliseen المُخلَصِينَ	8	4	**37:74**

Now, consider the words *"Mukhlis," "Mukhliseen,"* and *"Al-Mukhliseen."* The occurrence of *"Mukhlis"* in the Quran totals 20 times, with Verse 37:74 serving as its midpoint. Similarly, *"Mukhliseen"* appears 15 times, and *"Al-Mukhliseen"* 8 times, with Verse **37:74** remaining central in both cases.

All Occurences of

Mukhlis مُخلَص

#	C		V
#1	2	:	139
#2	7	:	29
#3	10	:	22
#4	12	:	24
#5	15	:	40
#6	19	:	51
#7	29	:	65
#8	31	:	32
#9	37	:	40
#10	**37**	:	**74**
#11	37	:	128
#12	37	:	160
#13	37	:	169
#14	38	:	83
#15	39	:	2
#16	39	:	11
#17	39	:	14
#18	40	:	14
#19	40	:	65
#20	98	:	5

Mukhliseen مُخلَصِينَ

#	C		V
#1	7	:	29
#2	10	:	22
#3	12	:	24
#4	15	:	40
#5	29	:	65
#6	31	:	32
#7	37	:	40
#8	**37**	:	**74**
#9	37	:	128
#10	37	:	160
#11	37	:	169
#12	38	:	83
#13	40	:	14
#14	40	:	65
#15	98	:	5

Al Mukhliseen المُخلَصِينَ

#	C		V
#1	12	:	24
#2	15	:	40
#3	37	:	40
#4	**37**	:	**74**
#5	37	:	128
#6	37	:	160
#7	37	:	169
#8	38	:	83

Table 9.8: All occurrences in the Quran

That is, in the Quran, the words *"Mukhlis," "Mukhliseen,"* and *"Al-Mukhliseen"* before and after Chapter 37:74 appear 10 times, 7 times, and 4 times respectively, maintaining equal distribution on both sides. This uniform distribution again illustrates a methodical symmetry in the Quran's structure. *Table 9.8* shows all the occurrences of the words *"Mukhlis," "Mukhliseen,"* and *"Al-Mukhliseen."*

***

The Center Verse 7:31 - Example #9

WORD / PHRASE	No. of Times	Half / Mid	Mid Verse
Adam أَدَمَ	25	13	**7:31**
Bani Adam بَنِى أَدَمَ	8	4	**7:31**
Ya Bani Adam يٰبَنِى أَدَمَ	5	3	**7:31**

The names *"Adam," "Bani Adam,"* and *"Ya Bani Adam"* also exhibit a remarkable balance in their occurrences. "Adam" appears 25 times, with Verse 7:31 as its midpoint. Likewise, *"Bani Adam"* appears 8 times, and *"Ya Bani Adam"* 5 times, with Verse **7:31** maintaining their central position.

So, in the Quran, the names *"Adam," "Bani Adam,"* and *"Ya Bani Adam"* before and after Chapter 7:31 appear equally, 12 times, 4 times, and 2 times, respectively.

This careful arrangement ensures uniformity in representing these names throughout the Quran. *Table 9.9* shows all the occurrences of the words *"Adam," "Bani Adam,"* and *"Ya Bani Adam"*.

All Occurences of

Adam أَدَمَ

#	C	:	V
#1	2	:	31
#2	2	:	33
#3	2	:	34
#4	2	:	35
#5	2	:	37
#6	3	:	33
#7	3	:	59
#8	5	:	27
#9	7	:	11
#10	7	:	19
#11	7	:	26
#12	7	:	27
#13	**7**	**:**	**31**
#14	7	:	35
#15	7	:	172
#16	17	:	61
#17	17	:	70
#18	18	:	50
#19	19	:	58
#20	20	:	115
#21	20	:	116
#22	20	:	117
#23	20	:	120
#24	20	:	121
#25	36	:	60

Bani Adam بَنِى أَدَمَ

#	C	:	V
#1	5	:	27
#2	7	:	26
#3	7	:	27
#4	**7**	**:**	**31**
#5	7	:	35
#6	7	:	172
#7	17	:	70
#8	36	:	60

Ya Bani Adam يَبَنِى أَدَمَ

#	C	:	V
#1	7	:	26
#2	7	:	27
#3	**7**	**:**	**31**
#4	7	:	35
#5	36	:	60

Table 9.9: All occurrences in the Quran

* * *

The Center Verse 6:95 - Example #10

WORD / PHRASE	No. of Times	Half / Mid	Mid Verse
Life الحَىَّ	12	6	**6:95**
Death المَيِّتِ	12	6	**6:95**

Finally, let's explore the words *"Al Hayy"* (the Living) and *"Al Mayyat"* (the Dead). Both words appear 12 times each in the Quran, with Verse **6:95** as their midpoint. This perfection further demonstrates the Quran's meticulous balance, as they appear an equal number of times before and after this pivotal verse 6:95. The words *"Al Hayy"* and *"Al Mayyat"*appear equally, 6 times each, before and after Verse 6:95

Moreover, the equal frequency of *"Al Hayy"* and *"Al Mayyat"*, totalling 12 times each, throughout the Quran highlights the precision in the distribution of these contrasting yet corresponding concepts.

Table 9.10 shows all the occurrences of the words *"Al Hayy"* (Life) and *"Al Mayyat"* (Death).

All Occurences of

Life الحَيّ

	C	V		C	V
#1	2	255	#7	10	31
#2	3	2	#8	2nd time	
#3	3	27	#9	25	58
#4	2nd time		#10	30	19
#5	6	95	#11	2nd time	
#6	**6**	**95**	**#12**	40	65
	(2nd time)				

Death المَيِّتِ

	C	V		C	V
#1	2	173	#7	10	31
#2	3	27	#8	2nd time	
#3	2nd time		#9	16	115
#4	5	3	#10	30	19
#5	6	95	#11	2nd time	
#6	**6**	**95**	**#12**	36	33
	(2nd time)				

Table 9.10

- Furthermore, the difference between the first (2:255) and last (40:65) occurrences of the word *"Al Hayy"* is noteworthy. The difference between their chapter numbers (40 – 2) is equal to **38** and the difference between their verse numbers (255 – 65) equals **190.** Both 38 and 190 are perfect multiples of 19.
- Even the first mention (2:173) of the word *"Al Mayyat"* exhibits a calculation of the number 19. The difference between the chapter number and verse number (173 -2) equals **171** (19 x 9), and the

sum of the first chapter number (2) and the last chapter number (36), equals **38**, a multiple of 19.

* * *

In each of the examples cited, the Quran reveals a profound symmetry of words that surpasses human authorship or ordinary compilation, providing compelling evidence of its divine origin. There are other examples as well that demonstrate a balanced occurrence of certain words. For instance, the word *"Zikrillah"* appears 38 times, while *"Al-Absaar"* appears 17 times in the Quran. Verse **24:37** serves as a midpoint for these occurrences. This means from the beginning of the Quran up to verse 24:37, *"Zikrillah"* appears 19 times and *"Al-Absaar"* appears 8 times. After verse 24:37, *"Zikrillah"* appears exactly 19 times again, and *"Al-Absaar"* appears 8 times. Verse 24:37 splits the words *"Zikrillah"* and *"Al-Absaar"* into equal halves.

As we unravel its mysteries, we are reminded of the ceaseless mathematics encoded within its verses. The symmetrical distribution of words and names across its verses exhibits the Quran's miraculous composition and compilation, leaving even the staunchest critics in awe of its profound symmetry.

10

THE PRECISE CALCULATION IN NAMES OF PROPHETS

Whenever and wherever Mathematics strikes, history automatically loses its control and dominion. Our discussion and mission would remain incomplete if we omitted the names of the Prophets in our analysis. Out of 1,24,000 prophets, about 27 names of prophets are mentioned in the Quran. Yet, it is not merely the presence of these chosen names but the mathematical symphony underlying their occurrences that speaks volumes about the Quran's divine origin and compilation.

In the Quran, various prophets are mentioned with varying frequencies, some appearing numerous times, others only a couple of times, and some even an equal number of times. This pattern is intriguing, suggesting a deliberate design in the text's composition. For instance, prominent prophets like Moses and Abraham are mentioned frequently, while others, like Ishmael and Idris, are referenced less often. The repetition of their names is not arbitrary; rather, it is purposeful, and this invites a deeper investigation into whether there is a mathematical structure underlying these occurrences.

Specifically, we can count and list the number of times each prophet is mentioned throughout the Quran to determine if these occurrences are connected to the number 19, which we have identified as the sign and the seal in the Quranic context. If the frequency of prophetic names aligns with this numerical pattern, it would strongly reinforce the argument that the Quran's structure is divinely inspired and mathematically precise. We will proceed by exploring the precise calculations embedded in the Quran, specifically regarding the names of the prophets.

The Chosen Names - Case #1

The first time a Prophet's name is mentioned in the Quran is Prophet *Adam*, in Chapter 2, verse 31, precisely the 38th line of the Quran. This computation of 38 includes the 7 lines of Chapter 1. The significance lies in the fact that 38 is a multiple of 19, hinting at a deeper numerical harmony woven into the fabric of compilation.

(Quran 2:31) *He taught* **Adam** *the names of all things, then He presented them to the angels and said, "Tell Me the names of these, if what you say is true?"*

* * *

The mention of Prophet Moses follows, positioned 19 lines after Adam's mention in Chapter 2, verse 51, a numerical alignment that underscores the Quran's meticulous composition. This symmetry again highlights the deliberate arrangement of verses, reinforcing the Quran's divine composition.

(Quran 2:51) *And remember when We appointed forty nights for* ***Moses****, then you worshipped the calf in his absence, acting wrongfully.*

* * *

The last-mentioned prophet in the Quran is also Prophet Moses, in verse 19 of Chapter 87. This closure in verse number 19 echoes the mathematical consistency in the Quran.

(Quran 87:19) *The Scriptures of Abraham and* ***Moses****.*

The Chosen Names - Case #2

A few verses of the Quran: 2:133, 2:136, 2:140, 3:84, and 4:163 mention the names of 4 Prophets and align to the number 19. All five verses listed below mention together the names of four prophets - *Ibrahim, Ismail, Ishaq, and Yaqub* - in the entire verse or in a group within the verse. The total occurrence of these four names (69 + 12 + 17 + 16) throughout the Quran is **114**, a multiple of 19 (6 x 19). *Refer to Table 10.1* showing the names of 4 Prophets and the frequency of their names in the Quran.

Sr.	Names of Prophets			No. of
No.	Name	Biblical	Arabic	Times
#1	Ibrahim	(Abraham)	إبرٰهيم	69
#2	Ismail	(Ishmael)	إسمٰعيل	12
#3	Ishaq	(Isaac)	إسحٰق	17
#4	Yaqub	(Jacob)	يَعقوب	16
		TOTAL		**114**

Table 10.1: *Total occurrence of the Names of four Prophets*

All five verses that mention together the names of four prophets are:

(Quran 2:133) *Or did you witness when death came to* ***Jacob?*** *He asked his children, "Who will you worship after my passing?" They replied, "We will ˹continue to˺ worship your God, the God of your forefathers,* ***Abraham, Ishmael, and Isaac,*** *the One God. And to Him we ˹all˺ submit."*

(Quran 2:136) *Say, O believers, "We believe in God and what has been revealed to us; and what was revealed to* ***Abraham, Ishmael, Isaac, Jacob,*** *and his descendants; and what was given to Moses, Jesus, and other prophets from their Lord. We make no distinction between any of them. And to God we all submit."*

(Quran 2:140) *Do you claim that* ***Abraham, Ishmael, Isaac, Jacob****, and his descendants were all Jews or Christians?" Say, "Who is more knowledgeable: you or God?" Who does more wrong than those who hide the testimony they received from God? And God is never unaware of what you do.*

(Quran 3:84) *Say, O Prophet, "We believe in God and what has been revealed to us and what was revealed to* ***Abraham, Ishmael, Isaac, Jacob****, and his descendants; and what was given to Moses, Jesus, and other prophets from their Lord, we make no distinction between any of them, and to Him we fully submit."*

(Quran 4:163) *Indeed, We have sent revelation to you O Prophet as We sent revelation to Noah and the prophets after him. We also sent revelation to* ***Abraham, Ishmael, Isaac, Jacob****, and his descendants, as well as Jesus, Job, Jonah, Aaron, and Solomon. And to David, We gave the Psalms.*

* * *

Another verse of the *Quran:* 6:84 mentions the names of 3 Prophets and aligns to the number 19.

Quran 6:84 mentions together the names of three prophets - *Ishaq, Yaqub, and Nuh* - in continuity. The total occurrence of these names throughout the Quran is **76**, a multiple of 19 (4 x 19), further consolidating our claim about the unique composition of the Quran.

Remarkably, the appended number, **684**, is also a multiple of the number 19 (36 x 19). *Refer to Table 10.2* showing the names of 3 Prophets and the frequency of their names in the Quran.

Sr. No.	Names of Prophets Name	Biblical	Arabic	No. of Times
#1	Ishaq	(Isaac)	إسحٰق	17
#2	Yaqub	(Jacob)	يَعقوب	16
#3	Nuh	(Noah)	نوح	43
		TOTAL		**76**

Table 10.2: Names of Prophets in Verse 6:84

Another interesting point is that, in continuation, verse 6:83 mentions the name of 1 Prophet *(Ibrahim)* only, while verse 6:84 mentions the names of 9 prophets *(Ishaq, Yaqub, Nuh, Dawud, Sulayman, Ayyub, Yusuf, Musa, Harun)*. The distribution of these names in the ratio **1:9** forms the intriguing pattern that again leads us to the number 19.

(Quran 6:83) *This was the argument We gave* ***Abraham*** *against his people. We elevate in rank whoever We please. Surely your Lord is All-Wise, All-Knowing.*

(Quran 6:84) *And We blessed him with* ***Isaac*** *and* ***Jacob****. We guided them all as We previously guided* ***Noah*** *and those among his descendants:* ***David, Solomon, Job, Joseph, Moses,*** *and* ***Aaron.*** *This is how We reward the good-doers.*

* * *

Three consecutive verses of the *Quran* 6:84, 6:85, 6:86 mention the names of 17 Prophets and align to the number 19.

In three consecutive verses 6:84, 6:85, and 6:86 of the Quran, the names of 17 prophets are mentioned together. The total occurrence of these names throughout the Quran is **380**, a multiple of 19 (20 x 19). The names of 17 Prophets and the frequency of their names in the Quran are shown in *Table 10.3*

* * *

Sr.	Names of Prophets			No. of
No.	Name	Biblical	Arabic	Times
#1	Ishaq	(Isaac)	إسحٰق	17
#2	Yaqub	(Jacob)	يَعقوب	16
#3	Nuh	(Noah)	نوح	43
#4	Dawud	(David)	داوۥد	16
#5	Sulayman	(Solomon)	سُلَيمٰن	17
#6	Ayyub	(Job)	أَيّوب	4
#7	Yusuf	(Joseph)	يوسُف	27
#8	Musa	(Moses)	موسىٰ	136
#9	Harun	(Aaron)	هٰرون	20
#10	Zakariya	(Zachariah)	زَكَرِيّا	7
#11	Yahya	(John the Baptist)	يَحيىٰ	5
#12	Isa	(Jesus)	عيسىٰ	25
#13	Ilias	(Elias)	إلياس	2
#14	Ismail	(Ishmael)	إسمٰعيل	12
#15	Alyasa	(Elisha)	اليَسَعَ	2
#16	Yunus	(Jonah)	يونُس	4
#17	Lut	(Lot)	لوط	27
	TOTAL			**380**

Table 10.3

All these examples undoubtedly reveal a consistency that exceeds human comprehension. The consistent appearance of the number 19 in the names of the Prophets is another layer of evidence supporting the idea that the Quran's composition is far from random.

The Chosen Names - Case #3

Prophet *"Adam"* أدَم and *"Esa"* (Jesus) عيسى are mentioned an equal number of times in the Quran. While comparing *Esa* and *Adam* in the Quran 3:59, God says:

> إِنَّ مَثَلَ عِيسَىٰ عِندَ اللَّهِ كَمَثَلِ آدَمَ خَلَقَهُ مِن تُرَابٍ ثُمَّ قَالَ لَهُ كُن فَيَكُونُ ۝
>
> (Quran 3:59) *Indeed, the example of* ***Jesus*** *in the sight of God* ***is the same*** *as that of* ***Adam***. *He created him from dust, then said to him, "Be!" And he was!*

The principle of equivalence between *Esa* and *Adam*, in the sight of God, is emphasized in verse 3:59. Remarkably, the Quran treats the names of *Adam* and *Esa* equally, with both names appearing 25 times each in the sacred text. *Refer to Table 10.4.* showing all occurrences of the names of *Adam* and *Esa* (Jesus) in the Quran.

All Occurences of

Adam ادَمَ

	C		V		C		V
#1	2	:	31	#13	7	:	31
#2	2	:	33	#14	7	:	35
#3	2	:	34	#15	7	:	172
#4	2	:	35	#16	17	:	61
#5	2	:	37	#17	17	:	70
#6	3	:	33	#18	18	:	50
#7	**3**	**:**	**59**	**#19**	**19**	**:**	**58**
#8	5	:	27	#20	20	:	115
#9	7	:	11	#21	20	:	116
#10	7	:	19	#22	20	:	117
#11	7	:	26	#23	20	:	120
#12	7	:	27	#24	20	:	121
				#25	36	:	60

Esa عيسىٰ

	C		V		C		V
#1	2	:	87	#13	5	:	78
#2	2	:	136	#14	5	:	110
#3	2	:	253	#15	5	:	112
#4	3	:	45	#16	5	:	114
#5	3	:	52	#17	5	:	116
#6	3	:	55	#18	6	:	85
#7	**3**	**:**	**59**	**#19**	**19**	**:**	**34**
#8	3	:	84	#20	33	:	7
#9	4	:	157	#21	42	:	13
#10	4	:	163	#22	43	:	63
#11	4	:	171	#23	57	:	27
#12	5	:	46	#24	61	:	6
				#25	61	:	14

Table 10.4

- The number **7** is emphasized throughout this verse. The 7th time the name of *Adam* and the 7th time the name of *Esa* (Jesus) is mentioned is in the same location, which is 3:59.
- Even the sum (3+5+9) of the digits of 3:59 is equal to **17**, which mathematically is the 7th prime number.
- The names of Prophets **أدَمْ** *Adam* and **عيسى** *Esa* (Jesus) together have **7** Arabic letters (3 + 4).
- In Chapter 7, the name of *Adam* appears **7** times.
- *Table 10.4* shows 50 verses. One verse (3:59) is common to both names, so the total number of verses in the Quran that mention the names أدَمْ Adam and عيسى Esa is **49**, which is the square of 7.
- Even the verses before and after verse 3:59 contain **7** words. That is, both verses 3:58 and 3:60 contain 7 words. Interestingly, writing the 3 verse numbers in sequence **585960** gives us a number that is a multiple of 19.
- The verse 3:59 has exactly **7** unique letters (**ب ت خ ر س ف و**).
- Letter **خ** is the center of the verse and is the **7th** letter of the *Hija'i* Arabic Alphabet.
- The letter "**ل**" is repeated the most in the verse, occurring **7** times.
- The 19th time both the names *Adam* and *Esa* are mentioned is in Chapter **19**.
- As stated before, the name of *Esa* appears 25 times in the Quran. Interestingly, the sum of the Chapter numbers (2, 3, 4, 5, 6, **19**, 33, 42, 43, 57, 61) where *Esa* is mentioned is equal to 275, which is a multiple of 25 (11 x 25). The center chapter of this group of chapters is Chapter **19**.

- The 25th time the names of *Adam* and *Esa* (Jesus) are mentioned is in verses 36:60 and 61:14, respectively. The sum of all the numbers of these two verses (36 + 60 + 61 + 14) is equal to **171**, a multiple of 19.

The Chosen Names - Case #4

In the grand narrative of the Quran, numbers whisper secrets, patterns emerge like constellations, and connections deepen beyond what the eye can see. Among these remarkable mathematics lies the numerical design surrounding the name of Prophet *Muhammed* (S) مُحَمَّد

Prophet *Muhammed* (S) is mentioned 4 times in the entire Quran at 3:144, 33:40, 47:2, and 48:29. The 47th chapter of the Quran bears his name: *Surah Muhammed,* containing **38** verses, a multiple of 19.

مُحَمَّد

- The name *Muhammed* has 3 unique Arabic letters **(م د ح)**, which are the 6th, 8th, and 24th letters of the Arabic Alphabet. The sum of (6 + 8 + 24) equals **38**, a multiple of 19.
- In *Surah Al Hamd*, the first chapter of the Quran, the three letters **(م د ح)** appear 5, 4, and 15 times, respectively. The appended number **5415** is perfectly divisible by 19. *Refer to Table 10.5*

Muhammed (S)					
	C		V	C+V	C-V
#1	3	:	144	147	**141**
#2	33	:	40	73	7
#3	47	:	2	49	45
#4	48	:	29	77	**19**

VISIBLE SEQUENCE

↓ 47 + 48 = **95** ÷ 19
← 928427404334413 ÷ **19**

(3144 - 3340 - 472 + 4829) = 4161 ÷ **19**

Table 10.5

- The first mention of *Muhammed* (S) appears in Chapter 3, Verse 144. At first glance, it may seem like just another reference. But mathematically, the difference between the chapter number (3) and verse number (144) is **141**, a number precisely divisible by 47, the chapter named after Prophet *Mumhammed (S)*.
- This verse 3:144 falls on the 437th line out of 6236 lines of the Quran, where **437** is a multiple of 19, a number that serves as a sign and the seal throughout the Quran's structure.
- The sum of the chapter numbers of the first two mentions (3 + 33) of the name *Muhammed (S)* equals **36**, pointing directly to Surah *Ya-Sin*, which again is a reference to Prophet *Muhammed (S)* and the combined number formed from the first two verses (**14440**), it remains divisible by 19.
- The sum of the chapter numbers of the last two occurrences (47 + 48) equals **95**, again a perfect multiple of 19.
- The beauty of this design deepens when we examine the sum of the products of the numbers in the first and last occurrence of his name: (3 × 144) + (48 × 29) = **1824**, a number flawlessly divisible by 19.
- And then comes the final touch, the last mention of *Muhammed (S)* appears in Chapter 48, Verse 29. If we subtract the chapter number from the verse number (48 - 29), the result is **19**, reaffirming the divine signature once again.
- Expressing the occurrences with operators (3144 - 3340 - 472 + 4829) equals **4161**, which is once again, exactly divisible by 19.
- Yet, the Quran does not stop here. The reverse of all the occurrences of the name *Muhammed (S)* forms the number **92842740433441 3**, perfectly divisible by 19.

- One more vital point, the name *"Ahmed"*, another reference to Prophet *Muhammed (S)* is in Chapter 61. This chapter contains 14 verses, and when we subtract the total verses from the chapter number (61 - 14), the result is **47**, pointing straight back to Surah *Muhammed!*

The Chosen Names - Case #5

Every chapter and every story of the Quran has a hidden mathematical pattern. And some stories, like that of Prophet *Yusuf* (Joseph), are timeless in wisdom and astonishing in mathematical design.

Nested within the folds of the Quran is Chapter 12, *Surah Yusuf*, which is the chapter named after Prophet *Yusuf*. A chapter famed for its enchanting story and profound emotions of the 12 brothers. But as the words unfold, something extraordinary lies beneath, mathematics quietly at work, weaving its own layer of the tale.

The name *"Yusuf"* is mentioned exactly 27 times across the Quran, but curiously, in 26 different verses. That may seem trivial until we find that the midpoint of these 26 verses is **12:56**. Verse 12:56 acts as the anchor of the chapter. *Refer to Table 10.6:*

Even more stunning, 24 of those 26 mentions occur inside *Surah Yusuf* itself. And yet again, the middle mention within the chapter, like a well-balanced scale, is found in verse **12:56**. This verse is no ordinary line; it happens to contain the 12th time the name "*Yusuf*" is mentioned, and it is the middle verse of the 12th Chapter, the 56th verse out of the chapter's total 111 verses, making it the central verse of *Surah Yusuf*. Everything seems to revolve around 12:56. The first 2 lines (Line 1, 2) of Chapter 12 contain 5 and 6 words respectively, forming the number 56.

Yusuf in Quran يوسُف							
	C		V		C		V
#1	6	:	84	#14	12	:	58
#2	12	:	4	#15	12	:	69
#3	12	:	7	#16	12	:	76
#4	12	:	8	#17	12	:	77
#5	12	:	9	#18	12	:	80
#6	12	:	10	#19	12	:	84
#7	12	:	11	#20	12	:	85
#8	12	:	17	#21	12	:	87
#9	12	:	21	#22	12	:	89
#10	12		29	#23	**12**	:	**90**
#11	12	:	46	#24	12	:	94
#12	12	:	51	#25	12	:	99
#13	12	:	56	#26	40	:	34

Yusuf in Chp. 12 يوسُف							
	C		V		C		V
#1	12	:	4	#13	12	:	58
#2	12	:	7	#14	12	:	69
#3	12	:	8	#15	12	:	76
#4	12	:	9	#16	12	:	77
#5	12	:	10	#17	12	:	80
#6	12	:	11	#18	12	:	84
#7	12	:	17	#19	12	:	85
#8	12	:	21	#20	12	:	87
#9	12		29	#21	12	:	89
#10	12	:	46	#22	12	:	90
#11	12	:	51	#23	12	:	94
#12	12	:	56	#24	12	:	99

Table 10.6

But this verse 12:56, which has 17 words, holds more than just the name of *Yusuf.* It also has the 17th occurrence of the word مُحسِنين *(Mohsineen),* a title given to those who do good. The word *"Mohsineen"* appears 33 times in the Quran, across 17 chapters, and its 17th appearance, which is also the midpoint of the occurrences of the word *"Mohsineen"*, lands at **12:56**. In Chapter 12, the word *"Mohsineen"* appears 5 times in verses 22, 36, 56, 78, and 90. Again, the center verse is 12:56. How perfect is this symmetry? Almost too perfect for a chance.

The only verse where Prophet *Yusuf's* name appears twice is 12:90. The 19th occurrence of the word *"Mohsineen"* in the Quran is also at 12:90.

The first 3 times *Yusuf* is mentioned are in Verse 4, 7, and 8; its mirror number **874** is a multiple of 19.

In the Quran, the first mention of *Yusuf is* in Chapter 6, verse 84 - that's **684**, again a multiple of 19 (19 × 36). In Chapter 12, the story begins with the first mention of *Yusuf* in Verse 4 and the last mention in Verse 99. The difference between the two verses (99 - 4) equals **95**, again a multiple of 19.

The difference between the total Verses of the chapter and the last mention of Prophet *Yusuf* is (111 – 99), which equals **12**. This indicates that the last 12 lines of chapter 12 do not contain the name *Yusuf.*

Verses 12 and 63 of chapter 12 - *Surah Yusuf*, end with the phrase "*wa inna lahu la haafizoon*" which means "And we will be his guardian". Combining the verse numbers with the Chapter number results in **126312**, which is a perfect multiple of 19.

There are 5 verses in the chapter, containing a total of 19 words. The verses are 24, 26, 32, 41, and 110. The combined number generated from them, **24263241110**, is perfectly divisible by 19.

The story of *Yusuf* isn't just beautiful in emotion; it is breathtaking in its mathematical design.

Thus, the precise calculation in the names of the Prophets emphasizes the Quran's mathematical intricacies, surpassing coincidence and reinforcing the Quran's claim of being a complete and meticulously preserved text that is impossible to replicate by human capabilities.

11

THE SIGNATURE OF GOD

With the passing of time, history has woven tales both true and tainted. In our quest to separate the wheat from the chaff, mathematics emerges as a beacon of clarity amidst the fog of deception. Mathematics stands as a steadfast guardian of truth against time.

The "Signature of God", etched in the language of mathematics, is visible throughout nature, reflected in the patterns, proportions, and designs of creation. From the scales of pinecones to the arrangement of seeds in a sunflower, there is an undeniable order that points to a deliberate design. This signature is evident in the balance and patterns of the natural world. Could it be that God used a specific ratio or formula to imprint this divine order? Many believe the answer lies in the precision of the universe, where even the smallest details follow a profound and purposeful design, perhaps God's way of signing His creation.

As we venture into the realm of divine composition and compilation marked by the signature of God, we uncover stunning and enigmatic mathematical concepts, including the Golden Ratio and the Fibonacci Series. Many people wonder whether the Golden ratio exists in the real world or is just as elusive as the elixir of life. Is there truly a sacred formula that governs everything?

The Golden Ratio

A fascinating mathematical concept that has intrigued mathematicians, artists, and scientists for centuries is the Golden Ratio. It is a special number that is approximately equal to **1.618**. It is often represented by the Greek letter *phi* Φ. The Golden Ratio can be found in nature, art, and architecture, and has been extensively studied for its mathematical properties and aesthetic appeal. Its profound presence can be seen in the shape of seashells, the arrangement of leaves on a stem, and the structure of human bodies.

There has been a belief since ancient times that creation follows a mathematical pattern, such as *phi* or the golden ratio. The Golden Ratio 1.618 is often referred to as the Divine Proportion, because of its seemingly magical properties. There are intricate designs in nature and the universe that reveal a divine signature, which many believe is the handiwork of God. To fully appreciate the Golden Ratio, it is important to understand the Fibonacci sequence and its close relation to the Golden Ratio.

The Fibonacci sequence

A series of numbers in which each number is the sum of the previous two numbers is called the Fibonacci sequence. The simplest is the series:

1, 1, 2, 3, 5, 8, 13, 21, 34, 55, 89, 144, 233, 377, 610, 987, 1597...

For example, (13+21)=34, (21+34)=55, (34+55)=89 and so on. The numbers that are part of the Fibonacci sequence are called Fibonacci numbers.

There is a remarkable and unexpected connection between the Golden Ratio and the Fibonacci. When we divide any number in the Fibonacci sequence by its preceding number, and as we keep doing this further on the sequence, we get a value that seems to get closer and closer to the Golden Ratio. For example, if you divide 233 by 144 or 610 by 377 or 1597 by 987, we get 1.618, which is a close approximation of the Golden Ratio. It is quite astounding that this famous irrational number *phi* is closely linked to a completely separate but equally famous sequence of whole numbers – the Fibonacci sequence.

Fibonacci's Whisper to 19

As one begins to follow the golden trail of the numbers in the Fibonacci series, we trace the early footprints in the sequence -1, 2, 3, 5. When placed side by side to form 1235, it gives rise to something stunning, a number divisible by 19.

Almost as if the universe has left a breadcrumb for the seeker, we venture further, and more signs emerge. Add the next cluster of four numbers in the sequence - 8, 13, 21, and 34 - and their total becomes 76, another number that leans towards 19, evenly, quietly, precisely.

Start from the beginning of the sequence – 1, 1, 2, 3, 5, 8, 13, 21, when placed together, forms **1123581321**, perfectly divisible by 19. Expunge the number 1 from both sides, and voila, **12358132**, again divisible by 19. Consider the last four digits 8132, a multiple of 19.

The harmony deepens when you glance at this stretch 5, 8, 13, 21, 34 -an uninterrupted chain of five Fibonacci numbers. String them together like pearls on a thread: **58132134** and voila. To the casual observer, it appears to be just a string of digits, but to the attuned mind, another nod to 19, another perfect multiple of the number 19.

The higher values in the sequence offer one more proof. Add 987 and 1597 - two peaks in this mathematical crescendo, and you get **2584**, a multiple of 19. Yet again, 19 stands behind the curtain, revealing itself in silence. Thus, the number 19 echoes within the beginning of the golden ladder of Fibonacci. If 1.618 is the golden ratio, then 19 is certainly the golden number within the Fibonacci sequence.

Probing further into the Fibonacci sequence, its presence in the Quran, and its relationship with the paramount number 19. In the heart of the Quran's verses, the Fibonacci sequence reveals its secret waggle dance.

The symmetrical number 5757

A series of numbers emerges when each chapter and verse number in the Quran is appended together. From this emerged list, we obtain 14 Fibonacci numbers (13, 21, 34, 55, 89, 144, 233) and (233, 377, 377, 610, 987, 987, 1597) as shown in *Table 11.1.*

Fibonacci Numbers in the Quran

	Sorted List				Ch.No. ⊕ V. No.		Sorted List				Ch.No. ⊕ V. No.
	C		V		Fibonacci		C		V		Fibonacci
#1	1	:	3	⊕	13	#8	23	:	3	⊕	233
#2	2	:	1	⊕	21	#9	3	:	77	⊕	377
#3	3	:	4	⊕	34	#10	37	:	7	⊕	377
#4	5	:	5	⊕	55	#11	6	:	10	⊕	610
#5	8	:	9	⊕	89	#12	9	:	87	⊕	987
#6	14	:	4	⊕	144	#13	98	:	7	⊕	987
#7	2	:	33	⊕	233	#14	15	:	97	⊕	1597
	TOTAL			Σ	**589** *(19 x 31)*		TOTAL			Σ	**5168** *(19 x 272)*

TOTAL (589 + 5168) = **5757** *(19 X 303)*

Table 11.1

When we split the list in half, the first 7 Fibonacci numbers sum to **589**, a perfect multiple of 19. The second half, comprising the remaining 7 Fibonacci numbers, totals **5168**, another number perfectly divisible by 19. This consistency is remarkable, as it indicates a deliberate mathematical structure. But the most profound revelation comes when we sum all 14 Fibonacci numbers from the appended column. The result is **5757**, a number both familiar and profound. The number 5757 resonates with symmetry and divides perfectly by the predominant number 19. The number 5757 is not alien to us.

- Dividing the 114 chapters of the Quran into two parts gives us a distribution of 57:57 chapters.
- Furthermore, the number of ODD and EVEN chapters in the Quran is equally divided, resulting in a perfect balance of 57:57. *(as explained in Chapter 6).*

Analysis of 6236

The Quran contains 6236 verses. At first glance, this number might appear ordinary, for it is not divisible by 19. Yet, 6236 is a special number and carries its own significance, for hidden within this number lie remarkable connections and correlations.

- The first 3 chapters of the Quran consist of 7, 200, and 286 verses. Applying math operators to these numbers along with the total verses in the Quran (6236), the result is **5757**, divisible by 19.

6236 + (7 - 286 - 200)	= **5757**	*(divisible by **19**)*

- If the total number of verses in the last 3 chapters of the Quran (4, 5, 6) is added to the total verses in the Quran (6236), the result is 6251, where **456** (19 x 24) and **6251**(19 x 329) are both multiples of 19.

6236 + (4+5+6)	= **6251**	*(divisible by **19**)*

- If the first 3 digits (623) of the total verses of the Quran (6236) are added to the total verses, we get **6859**, a veiled number not only divisible by 19 but is the cube of 19, represented as **(19 x 19 x 19).**

6236 + (623)	= 6859	(divisible by 19)

- If the center 2 digits (23) of the total verses of the Quran (6236) are subtracted from the total verses, we get **6213**, divisible by 19.

6236 - (23)	= 6213	(divisible by 19)

- If total verses of the Quran (6236) are multiplied by the Golden Ratio 1.618, we get **10089**, which is a perfect multiple of 19.

6236 x 1.618	= 10089	(divisible by 19)

What makes the finding about the Golden Ratio and the Fibonacci numbers within the Quran truly astounding is that these mathematical concepts and their specific placements serve as evidence that possibly the entire text has been compiled, preserved and unchanged for over fourteen centuries.

* * *

Surah Ar-Rahman

Chapter 55, named *Ar-Rahman,* might be the perfect example of the Golden Ratio and the Fibonacci Sequence intertwined within the Chapter's composition.

Amidst the pages of the Quran, not only a masterpiece of language but also of mathematical precision lies Surah *Ar-Rahman*, which is Chapter Number 55 of the Quran and has 78 verses. The Chapter is the epitome of numerical elegance. Number 55 is a part of the Fibonacci series, and the number 78 is formed by the Prime numbers (2 x 3 x 13), again, all numbers of the Fibonacci series. If we add the numbers 55 and 78, we get **133**, which is a multiple of 19.

The first verse - 55:1 *Ar-Rahman* ۞ is the same as the chapter name. When combined with the Chapter number, it forms the number **551**, which is again a multiple of the paramount number 19.

The Repeated Verse

Within the verses of *Surah ar-Rahman*, a symphony of numbers unfolds. At the heart of this symphony lies a repeated catchphrase, echoing the eternal question, "Then which of the favors of your Lord will you deny?" فَبِأَيِّ الَآ رَبِّكُمَا تُكَذِّبَانِ *[Fabi-ayyi aala-i rabbikuma tukazzibaan]*. Repeated not once or twice, but 31 times, this verse shapes its way through the mosaic of *Surah ar-Rahman*. Yet, amidst its repetitions lies a hidden pattern - a numerical code that speaks about a divine composition.

Verses 13, 21, 34, and 55, each a number of the sacred Fibonacci sequence as well, all contain the repeated verse, "Then which of the favors of your Lord will you deny?" فَبِأَيِّ الَآ رَبِّكُمَا تُكَذِّبَانِ . When these numbers are combined, a surprise unfolds: the number **13213455** is perfectly divisible by 19. Within this number 1**32**13**45**5, two other numbers are concealed, numbers 32 and 45, both of which also refer to verses 32 and 45, the same repeated verse, "Then which of the favors of your Lord will you deny?" فَبِأَيِّ الَآ رَبِّكُمَا تُكَذِّبَانِ ۞

And if numbers within the golden ratio (1.618) reveal themselves, verse numbers 16 and 18 both bear the same repeated verse, "Then which of the favors of your Lord will you deny?" فَبِأَيِّ الَآ رَبِّكُمَا تُكَذِّبَانِ . Within the golden ratio 1.**61**8, the number **61** hides itself. Yet again, verse 61 of *Surah Rahman* bears the same repeated verse displaying a symphony of divine composition.

All these Verses **13, 21, 34, 55, 32, 45, 16, 18, 61** *are:*
فَبِأَيِّ آلَاءِ رَبِّكُمَا تُكَذِّبَانِ ۞

Yet, the mathematical wonders do not end there. Of the 78 verses of Surah Rahman, 47 are distinct, and 31 are repeated. When these numbers are appended, the result is **4731**, a multiple of the distinguished number 19. Of the 78 verses, 9 verses do not end with the letter **ن** leaving 69 verses that do. When combined, **969** is a perfect multiple of 19. The pattern deepens, within the 69 verses, 31 are the repeated verses. So, this bifurcation of 78 verses produces the sequence 9-31-38. When read together, 93138 is a multiple of 19.

Structure of The Repeated Verse

Furthermore, the structure of the repeated line, "فَبِأَيِّ آلَاءِ رَبِّكُمَا تُكَذِّبَانِ" also reflects the divine composition. The line is repeated 31 times, with the first instance starting at line number 13. Notably, 13 is a mirror number of 31, and the difference between 31 and 13 is 18, which also corresponds to the **18** letters in the line. Constructed with 18 letters in total, including 3 letters that are repeated and 8 that are unique, when combined, it highlights 38, a multiple of 19. Both the numbers 3 and 8 are also a part of the Fibonacci series. Additionally, when we consider the total occurrences of each of the 3 repeated letters, they form the number 532, which is also a multiple of 19. *Refer to Table 11.2*

	3 Repeated Letters			
	أ	ب	ك	
No. of Times	**5**	**3**	**2**	(÷ 19)

Table 11.2

The 8 unique (1), and 3 repeated letters recur as 1, 2, 3, or 5 times in ascending order. Interestingly, **1235** is also a multiple of the majestic number 19 and a part of the early Fibonacci sequence.

Recurrence of The Repeated Verse

There is just one more verse in the Quran that begins with the same words as *Fabi ayyi aala-i* (فَبِأَيِّ الآ), which can be found in Chapter 53: Verse 55 and reads:

53:55	فَبِأَيِّ الَآ رَبِّكَ تَتَمَارَىٰ	*Fabi-ayyi aala-i rabbika tatamaaraa*
"So which of the favors of your Lord will you dispute?"		
55:53	فَبِأَيِّ الَآ رَبِّكُمَا تُكَذِّبَانِ	*Fabi-ayyi aala-i rabbikuma tukazzibaan*
"So which of the favours of your Lord will you deny?"		

So, interestingly, verse number 53:55 in *Surah An-Najam* is the inverse of verse number 55:53 in *Surah Ar-Rahman*. Mathematically, the number **535553** is a multiple of the predominant number 19. *Refer to Table 11.3*

فَبِأَيِّ الَآ رَبِّكَ تَتَمَارَىٰ	فَبِأَيِّ الَآ رَبِّكُمَا تُكَذِّبَانِ
53:55	55:53
16 Letters	**18** Letters
1.618 Golden Ratio	

Table 11.3

Verse 53:55 has **16** letters, whereas 55:53 has **18** letters. If these two numbers are put together, they form the Golden Ratio **(1.618)**.

* * *

The Significance of 1.618 in Total Verse Numbers

The chapters of the Quran have varying lengths, with some containing just a few verses, while others stretch over many pages and have several verses. At first glance, these varying lengths might seem arbitrary, but upon deeper reflection, we begin to see a clear, deliberate design. The arrangement of chapters and verses is not random; rather, it follows a precise structure that hints at mathematical balance. From the number of verses in a chapter to the placement of chapters in the Quran, patterns such as the Golden Ratio, Fibonacci series, prime numbers, and other mathematical phenomena emerge.

The precise alignment of the total verse numbers of a chapter in the Quran with the total verse numbers of another chapter presents a fascinating case against the notion that the total number of verses in a chapter is arbitrary.

- For instance, Chapter 2, which contains 286 verses, aligns perfectly with another Chapter when the Golden Ratio is applied. When 286 is divided by 1.618, the result is 176, which remarkably corresponds to the exact number of verses in Chapter 4.
- Similarly, Chapter 3 contains 200 verses, and dividing 200 by 1.618 yields 123, which matches the number of verses in Chapter 11.

These patterns are not mere coincidences; they suggest an underlying mathematical structure within the Quran's composition. This intricate pattern continues, illustrating the Quran's alignment with the Golden Ratio. *Refer to Table 11.4*

- Chapter 20, for example, contains 135 verses. When we divide 135 by 1.618, we get 83, which corresponds exactly to the number of verses in Chapter 36.
- Similarly, Chapter 37 has 182 verses, and when this number is divided by the Golden Ratio, the result is 112, the precise number of verses in Chapter 21.
- The pattern doesn't stop there. Chapter 21 itself has 112 verses, and dividing this by 1.618 yields 69, which is the exact number of verses in Chapter 29.

Ch. No.	Verses	Golden Ratio		Verses	Ch. No.
Golden Ratio in Verses					
2	**286**	÷ 1.618	=	**176**	4
3	**200**	÷ 1.618	=	**123**	11
4	**176**	÷ 1.618	=	**109**	10
20	**135**	÷ 1.618	=	**83**	36
37	**182**	÷ 1.618	=	**112**	21
21	**112**	÷ 1.618	=	**69**	29

Table 11.4

These consistent correlations reveal a sophisticated numerical harmony within the Quran that aligns perfectly with the Golden Ratio, a mathematical constant often found in nature, art, and architecture.

Verse 16:18 and Golden Ratio 1.618

In our exploration of the Golden Ratio within the Quran, we encounter a profound example in verse 16:18. The Golden Ratio, represented by the number 1.618, has fascinated mathematicians, artists, and philosophers for centuries due to its occurrence in nature, art, and architecture. Its presence in the Quran, however, adds a layer of divine intricacy that invites deeper reflection. Verse 16:18 of the Quran reads,

15 x **1.618** = 24

← 15 → | ← 24 →

وَإِن تَعُدُّوا۟ نِعْمَةَ ٱللَّهِ لَا تُحْصُوهَآ ۗ إِنَّ ٱللَّهَ لَغَفُورٌ رَّحِيم

← 39 →

39 ÷ **1.618** = 24

Quran 16:18 *"If you try to* ***count*** *God's blessings, you would never be able to* ***number*** *them. Surely God is All-Forgiving, Most Merciful."*

This verse 16:18, which states directly about counting and numbering, inherently connects to the domain of mathematics.

- The verse contains 39 letters, divided into two distinct parts: the first with **24** letters and the second part with **15**. This division itself is not random but follows the Golden Ratio. When 39 is divided by 1.618, the result is 24, perfectly matching the number of letters in the first part.
- Furthermore, when 15 is multiplied by 1.618, the result is also 24, aligning with the structure of the verse. This demonstrates that the verse is constructed according to the Golden Ratio, embedded within its very letters.
- The verse is composed of 10 words, which are again split into two parts: the first segment with **6** words and the second with **4**. Remarkably, 10 divided by 1.618 equals 6, and 4 multiplied by 1.618 equals 6. This dual adherence to the Golden Ratio in both letters and words emphasizes the deliberate and intricate design of the verse.

The connections don't end there. The word *"Rahim"* (Most Merciful) within this verse holds a special significance. It is the center point of the 115 occurrences of the word *"Rahim"* in the Quran. Before and after verse **16:18**, *"Rahim"* is mentioned 57 times, that is, in the ratio of 57:57, where 57 is a multiple of 19, which reinforces the notion of the sign and the seal of the paramount and predominant number 19.

Chapters 16 and 18

In the golden weave of mathematics, when we multiply 16 and 18, two numbers close to the Golden Ratio, the result is 288. This number can be factored as 144 × 2, and both 144 and 2 are part of the Fibonacci sequence. Furthermore, if we add 16 and 18, we get 34, which is also a Fibonacci number. Even their difference, which is 2, belongs to the same sequence. This shows that the relationship between 16 and 18 is not only close to the Golden Ratio but also closely tied to the structure of the Fibonacci series.

To add more intrigue to the relationship between Chapter 16 and Chapter 18 in relation to the Quran, we scrutinize the mathematical connections that bind them.

Chapter 16, known as *Surah An-Nahl,* consists of **128** verses.

- When we add the chapter number to the number of verses (16 + 128), the sum is **144**, a number in the Fibonacci series.
- The difference between the chapter number (16) and the number of verses (128 – 16) is equal to **112**.
- When we multiply 144 by 112, the result is **16,128** - a number that intriguingly mirrors the appended chapter number (16) and the total number of verses (128).

144 x 112 = 16,128

Chapter 18, known as *Surah Al-Kahf,* which has 110 verses.

- Adding the chapter number to the number of verses (18 + 110) yields **128**, the exact number of verses found in Chapter 16.

This reciprocal relationship between the two chapters highlights a hidden symmetry, where the numbers not only align but also reinforce each other. The relationships between chapters and verses are imbued with mathematical precision, further suggesting that this arrangement is far from arbitrary.

* * *

Special Note: *The Arabic letter* ظ *appears only once in Chapter 54, in verse 31 and likewise, only once in Chapter 55, in verse 35. When these verse positions are read together as* ***3135****, the number is perfectly divisible* *by **19**, emphasizing the amazing numerical harmony in the Quran's structure.*

These examples collectively illustrate the profound mathematical structure embedded within the Quran, where the Golden Ratio, Fibonacci sequence, and numerical relationships between chapters create a tapestry of divine precision. This mathematical harmony within the Quran challenges the notion of coincidence and invites us to recognise the deliberate and intricate design that underpins the sacred text.

The golden ratio, revered throughout history as the divine proportion and the signature of God, reveals itself woven into the very fabric of the Quran's composition. It is the ratio upon which so many natural phenomena are based, the delicate spiral of seashells, the graceful curves of petals, and the proportions of the human body. And now, it emerges as a divine signature, etched into the numerical symphony of the Quran. The mathematics of the universe resonates within the verses of the Quran, affirming that the creator of the universe and the author of the Quran are one and the same.

As the symphony of numbers unfolds, Mathematics stands as the unwavering guardian of truth, illuminating the path of compilation against historical narrations. And in the background, 19 stands strong, once again affirming its role not just as a number, but as a guiding compass in a mathematically designed reality.

In the mathematical battle with the aid of the Fibonacci series, the Golden ratio, and the Golden number - 19, we find not only the truth of revelation but also the brilliant beauty of the divine proportion within the text of the Quran.

12

THE SILENT INTRUDER - DAGGER ALIF

The *'dagger alif'* is a short vertical stroke that appears above certain letters in the Arabic script. Placing the *'dagger alif'* above certain letters for pronunciation is the norm and is acceptable. However, introducing or replacing the *'dagger alif'* instead of the 'long vowel alif ' has resulted in a slight alteration in the way certain words were originally written in the Quran.

The journey to uncover the hidden layers within the Quran takes us deeper into history as we explore the intriguing concept of the *'dagger alif.'* The problem of the sharp projectile *'dagger alif'* introduced in the Quran is not merely a product of anyone's imagination, conjured from nowhere. To understand the *'dagger alif'* issue, we must research the archives of history, traveling back several centuries to the era of the Mamluk dynasty. This period is crucial for understanding ancient Arabic scripts and preserving the Quranic text.

The Mamluk Dynasty and Its Legacy

The Mamluk dynasty, which reigned from the 13th to the 16th centuries, is renowned for its cultural and intellectual achievements. Among these achievements is the creation of exquisite manuscripts, particularly of the Quran. One such manuscript, known as Sultan Baybar's Quran, stands out as a testament to the era's dedication to the preservation and beautification of the Quranic text.

Sultan Baybar's Quran

Housed in the British Library, Sultan Baybar's Quran is one of the most magnificent and meticulously crafted Quran from the Mamluk period. Created around 1305 AD in Cairo, this seven-volume manuscript is handwritten in gold, using a cursive Arabic script, typically reserved for ornamental headings. It is the earliest dated Quran of the Mamluk period, making it a precious artifact of historical and religious significance. The British Library has digitally preserved this impressive replica of the Holy Quran, available for online viewing to this day.

The manuscript from Sultan Baybar's Quran clears all doubts and depicts the original *"alif"* and the absence of the *'dagger alif'*, in contrast to the new scripts. *Refer to Fig 12.1,* where *"Aatayna"* and *"Sirat"* are spelt differently. In the new script, *"alif" is* replaced by *dagger alif*.

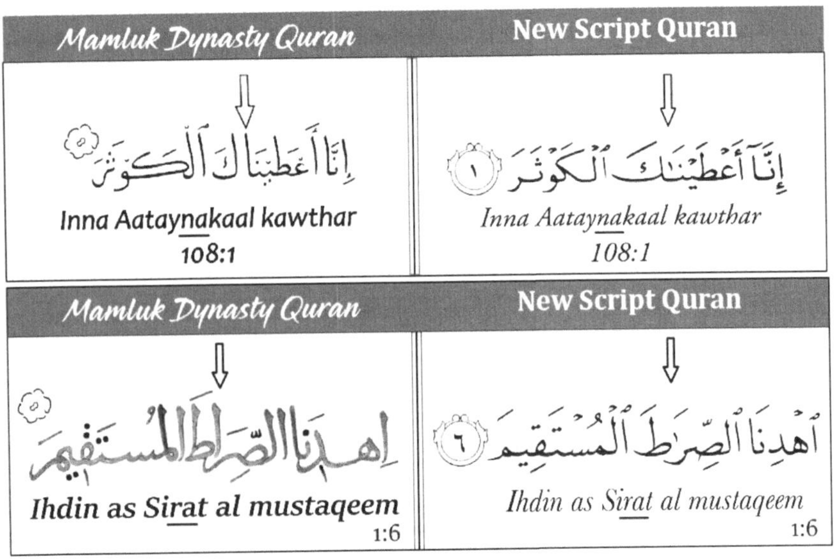

Figure 12.1

The Absence of the Dagger Alif

What makes Sultan Baybar's Quran particularly important to our discussion is the absence of the *'dagger alif'*. In this manuscript, wherever the *"alif"* originally existed, it still appears in its full form within the verses. This contrasts with later scripts where the *'dagger alif'* was introduced. This subtle yet significant change in the script prompts us to consider the implications of restoring the original *"alif"* when exploring the mathematical structures within the Quran. *Refer to Table 12.2,* where the original spelling of words is shown in contrast to the words spelt with a *dagger alif.*

✓	✗	✓	✗
Original	Dagger Alif	Original	Dagger Alif
الْعَالَمِينَ	ٱلْعَـٰلَمِينَ	أَعْطَيْنَاكَ	أَعْطَيْنَـٰكَ
صِرَاطَ	صِّرَٰطَ	الْكَافِرُونَ	ٱلْكَـٰفِرُونَ
مَالِكِ	مَـٰلِكِ	أَنْزَلْنَاهُ	أَنزَلْنَـٰهُ
كِتَاب	كِتَـٰب	السَّمَـوَاتِ	ٱلسَّمَـٰوَٰتِ

Table 12.2

Restoring the Original Alif

The *dagger alif* is perhaps the most understated yet devastating symbol embedded in the sacred text, serving as a substitution for the long vowel *alif.* Like a silent blade, it has pierced the Quranic script, not as a clarification, but as an invasive splinter, distorting the visibility of the Quran's mathematical purity.

If we aim to explore the mathematical patterns within the Quran, it is crucial to consider the original script. Restoring the substituted *'dagger alif* to its original full form of *"alif"* helps us maintain the integrity of the text and ensures that our analysis is based on the Quran as it was originally revealed. If left unchecked, it undermines the Quran's miraculous consistency, making it appear flawed to those seeking truth through numbers. Eliminating this silent invader is not an academic choice; it is a call to arms, a battle for preserving the Quran in its most exact, unblemished form.

The *dagger alif* problem is not about fonts; it must be addressed, **not as a minor correction**, but as a full-scale campaign. Restoring the original *"alif"* involves a careful examination of the text by those who are grounded in the Arabic language, comparing it with early manuscripts, having knowledge of the spellings of Arabic words, and identifying the places where the *'dagger alif'* was introduced. This process will not only enhance our appreciation of the divine composition but also ensure that the Quran remains intact and pure, as it was revealed to Prophet Muhammed (S), reaffirming its status as a miraculous text beyond human capability.

When we listen to the Quran today, we undoubtedly hear the same verses and words that were scripted in earlier times. However, what is written has been slightly revised according to the new scripts in terms of spelling. By restoring the original *"alif,"* we align the written text more closely with its recital form, preserving the scripted authenticity of the Quranic revelation.

13

THE SMALL CHAPTERS AND THE BIG CHALLENGE

History, clad in the armour of tradition and scholarship, stands resolute. However, mathematics, interwoven into the heart of the chapters, openly defies all notions of incompleteness or randomness in the Quran.

The Mathematical Challenge

The Quran presents a unique challenge to humanity: to produce a single chapter like it. This challenge is not limited to its linguistic beauty and profound meanings but also extends to its mathematical intricacies. Combining eloquence with mathematical precision, the Quran's divine composition makes it an unparalleled text beyond human capability. This challenge becomes especially evident when examining the mathematical patterns within the shortest chapters of the Quran.

Consider the task of writing a meaningful, rhyming chapter of just four lines while adhering to intricate mathematical constraints. For poets and authors, expressing thoughts and words with mathematical restrictions would be nearly impossible. Let's delve into the mathematics embedded in a few of the shortest chapters of the Quran to understand this challenge better.

The Challenge of Chapter 112: *Ahad* (The One)

This Chapter is a short declaration about God's absolute oneness, consisting of four lines.

Chapter - 112 - Ahad / Ikhlaas			
بِسْمِ ٱللَّهِ ٱلرَّحْمَـٰنِ ٱلرَّحِيمِ	**Lines**	**Letters**	**Words**
قُلْ هُوَ ٱللَّهُ أَحَدٌ ۞	1	11	4
ٱللَّهُ ٱلصَّمَدُ ۞	2	9	2
لَمْ يَلِدْ وَلَمْ يُولَدْ ۞	3	12	4
وَلَمْ يَكُن لَّهُۥ كُفُوًا أَحَدٌۢ ۞	4	15	5
TOTAL:	**4**	**47**	**15**

Quran: Chapter 112

Chapter Composition:

- The chapter consists of 4 lines.
- The chapter contains 47 letters.
- The chapter is made up of 13 different letters.
- The chapter contains 15 words.

The Dominance of the Number 4

Chapter 112, *Ahad* (The One), is a remarkable example of the Quran's inherent mathematics, with the number **4** prominently influencing its composition.

Structure of the Chapter

- The chapter has **4** lines.
- The 1st line and the 3rd line both contain **4** words.
- There are exactly **4** words in the chapter that consist of 4 letters.
- There are exactly **4** words in the chapter that consist of 2 letters.

- That chapter number 112 is perfectly divisible by **4** (28 x **4**).
- The digits of the chapter number 112 add (1 + 1 + 2) up to **4**.
- There are **4** dotted letters in the entire chapter: (ف ق ن ي)
- The chapter has **4** unique letters; used only once: (ص ف ق ن)
- The **4**th Line has 15 letters, which is the same as the total number of words (15) in the Chapter, and the number of letters in the chapter is 47, the 15th prime number.

Letters

- The 1st line contains **4** unique letters: (ح د ق و)
- The 2nd line contains **4** unique letters: (د ص م ه)
- The 3rd line has **4** occurrences of the letter "ل" (L)
- The 3rd line has **4** letters repeated twice: (د م و ي)
- The 4th line has **4** letters repeated twice: (ا ك ل و)
- The last letter of all **4** lines is "د", the 8th letter of the Arabic alphabet, and 8 is a multiple of **4**.
- The last line has 7 unique letters (ح د ف ق م ن ه ي), and 7 is the **4**th prime number.
- The letter "م" (M) appears **4** times in the Chapter.
- The letter "ه" (h) also appears **4** times in the Chapter.

Center of the Chapter - The letter "ل" (L)

- The letter "ل" is the center of the chapter, dividing the chapter into 23 letters before and 23 letters after it.
- Interestingly, the letter "ل" is the 23rd letter of the Arabic alphabet.
- "ل" is the only letter in the chapter with the vowel "*zer*" or "*kasrah*", the diagonal stroke below "لِ" makes it exceptional.
- The line with the center "ل" has **4** occurrences of the letter "ل".
- The line having the center "ل" has 12 letters, and "ل" appears 12 times in the chapter; 12 is a multiple of **4.**

- The center "ل" lies in the center of the word بَلَدْ
- The word بَلَدْ itself is the center of the chapter, dividing the chapter into 7 words before and 7 words after it.

Appended Letters and Words

- The total number of words in all 4 lines (4, 2, 4, 5) adds up to 15, and the number 4245 is divisible by 15.
- The total number of letters in all 4 lines (11, 9, 12, 15) adds up to 47, and the number 1191215 is divisible by 47.

Other References in the Quran

- Excluding Chapter 112, the total number of verses ending with the word *"Ahad"* أَحَد in the entire Quran is **4.**

	1	2	3	4
Verses	89:25	89:26	90:5	90:7

- Including Chapter 112, the chapters ending with the word *"Ahad"* أَحَد in the entire Quran are 89, 90, and 112. The combined number **8990112** is divisible by 4. The total of all the verse numbers (25 + 26 + 5 + 7 + 1 + 4) equals 68, which is also divisible by 4.
- Chapters ending with the letter "د" in the Quran are **4**.

	1	2	3	4
Chapters	50	111	112	113

Comparing with Chapter 1

- Chapter 1 *(Al-Hamd)* has **4** occurrences of the letter "د"
- If all the 13 letters used in Chapter 112 are counted within the 1st Chapter *(Al-Hamd)*, the total count is exactly 112, echoing the number of the Chapter- **112**. For example, the number of times the

letter أ *Alif* appears in Chapter *Al-Hamd* is 26, the number of times the letter "ح" appears is 5, the letter "د" appears is 4, and so on. *(Refer to Table 13.1).* This precise alignment could suggest that the placement of Chapter 112 within the Quran is not random but divinely orchestrated to be at 112.

Letters of Chapter 112 in Chapter 1

LETTER	CH. 1	LETTER	CH. 1	LETTER	CH. 1
ا	26	ق	1	ن	11
ح	5	ك	3	ه	5
د	4	ل	22	و	4
ص	2	م	15	ي	14
ف	0	TOTAL IN CHP. 1 =			112

Table 13.1

The Road to 19

- The first line 112:1 forms the number **1121**, which is divisible by 19. The third line 112:3, in reverse, forms the number 3211, which is also divisible by 19.
- In the first line, the number of Letters (11) appended to the number of words (4) gives **114**, a multiple of 19.
- Within the chapter, the number of letters from the first "ل" to the last "ل" is **38** letters, a multiple of 19.

The intricate mathematical design of Chapter 112, *Al Ahad* or *Al-Ikhlas*, highlights the Quran's divine composition, demonstrating that even its shortest chapters are beyond human capability to replicate. This level of complexity, design, and mathematical precision, combined with profound meaning and linguistic beauty, highlights the Quran's challenge to humanity to produce even one chapter like it.

* * *

The Challenge of Chapter 1: *Al-Fateha* (The Opener/ Key)

The complexities of the Quran intensify as we delve deeper into its smaller chapters. Chapter 1, *Al-Fateha* (The Opener), is a quintessential example of the Quran's inbuilt mathematics.

Previously, in Chapters 5 and 12 of this book, we discussed one of the subtleties introduced over time: the *'dagger alif'*, which replaced the original *"alif"* in many words. Recognizing and restoring these words to their original form is crucial for understanding the Quran's true mathematical patterns. In this chapter, *Al-Fateha*, we restore the original *"alif"* in the words **الْعَالَمِينَ** , **مَالِكِ** and **الصِّرَاط**.

CHAPTER 1 - AL-FATEHA الفاتحة	LINES	WORDS	LETTERS
بِسْمِ ٱللَّهِ ٱلرَّحْمَـٰنِ ٱلرَّحِيمِ ۞	1	4	19
الْحَمْدُ لِلَّهِ رَبِّ الْعَالَمِينَ ۞	2	4	18
الرَّحْمَنِ الرَّحِيمِ ۞	3	2	12
مَالِكِ يَوْمِ الدِّينِ ۞	4	3	12
إِيَّاكَ نَعْبُدُ وَإِيَّاكَ نَسْتَعِينُ ۞	5	4	19
اِهْدِنَا الصِّرَاطَ الْمُسْتَقِيمَ ۞	6	3	19
صِرَاطَ الَّذِينَ أَنْعَمْتَ عَلَيْهِمْ	7	9	44
غَيْرِ الْمَغْضُوبِ عَلَيْهِمْ وَلَا الضَّالِّينَ ۞			
TOTAL Σ **1**	**7**	**29**	**143**

Quran : Chapter 1

Chapter Composition:

- The chapter consists of 7 lines.
- There are 143 letters in the chapter.
- The chapter is made up of 21 different letters.
- The chapter contains 29 words.

The Dominance of the Numbers 7 and 19

Chapter 1, *Al-Fateha* (The Key), is a remarkable example of the Quran's mathematics, with the numbers 7 and 19 significantly shaping its composition.

Structure of the Chapter

- The chapter has **7** lines.
- The name *"Al-Fateha"* **الفاتِحَة** consists of **7** letters.
- The first line consists of 19 letters and is the most prominent line in the Quran. It consists of 4 words with the letter count of each word as 6, 6, 4, 3. The combined number 6643 is divisible by **7**.

19 Letters — 6 6 4 3

بِسْمِ اللَّهِ الرَّحْمَٰنِ الرَّحِيمِ

- The last line, verse 1:7 forms the number 17, which is the **7**th prime number. *Al-Fateha* is recited 17 times in the daily obligatory prayers.
- The chapter has **29** words. The difference in the digits of 29 (9 - 2) equals **7**.
- Out of the 28 letters in the Arabic alphabet, **21** are used in this chapter, a multiple of **7**, and the remaining **7** letters are not used.
- The **7** letters not used (**ث ج خ ز ش ظ ف**) are all dotted.
- The difference between the total number of letters (143) and words (29) is **114** (143 -29), which is divisible by 19, and also indirectly points towards the total number of Chapters in the Quran.

Dotted and Non-Dotted Letters

- The first line has **7** non-dotted letters. (**أ ح ر س ل م ه**)
- The third line has **7** letters. (**أ ح ر ل م ن ي**)

- The last line has **7** dotted letters. (ب ت ذ ض غ ن ي)
- Up to the third line, there are exactly **49** letters, which is expressed as **7** x **7** or the square of 7.
- The chapter contains 143 letters, out of which **38** are dotted letters, a multiple of 19, and without dots are **105** letters, a multiple of **7**.

End of Words and Lines

- Words ending in "**م**" are **7,** and Words ending in "**ن**" are **7**
- All lines end with either the letter "**م**" or "**ن**". The count of "**م**", appearing at the end of the line, is 3, and "**ن**" is 4, totalling **7**.
- The last line has 7 "**أ**" *(Alif)* and 7 "**ل**"

Complexity within Complexity

Verse 15:87 refers to Chapter #1 *Al-Fateha* as the "seven often-repeated verses," and this verse itself is a masterpiece of mathematical precision:

وَلَقَدْ ءَاتَيْنَٰكَ سَبْعًا مِّنَ ٱلْمَثَانِى وَٱلْقُرْءَانَ ٱلْعَظِيمَ ۝

*Certainly, We have given you the **seven** often-repeated verses and the great Quran **(15:87)***

- The verse **15:87** has exactly **7** words.
- The count and proportions of "**م**" and "**ن**" are the same, **3:4**, echoing the end segments of Chapter #1 *Al-Fateha*.
- The central word is "**من**" formed from both the key letters.
- The sum of the digits (1 + 5 + 8 + 7) is **21**, a multiple of **7**.
- The order of "**م**" and "**ن**" in the Arabic alphabet is the 24th and 25th letters respectively, summing to **49**, expressed as $(7)^2$.
- The verse is composed of **16** different letters, and the sum of its digits (1 + 6) is equal to **7**.

- Out of 16 letters, **7** are dotted (ب ت ث ظ ق ن ي)
- Out of 16 letters, 8 are unique letters and 8 are repeated letters.

Repetition and Uniqueness

- Out of 21 different letters used in Chapter *Al-Fateha*, 2 letters are unique and **19** are repeated in the chapter, highlighting the significance of 19.
- The 2 unique letters are the 21st letter "ق" and the 9th letter "ذ", summing to 30, the 19th composite number.

Mathematical Description

- *Al-Fateha* can also be described mathematically as Chapter 1 with 7 verses and 29 words. Appending these numbers (1, 7, 29) yields 1729, which is divisible by 19, and the digits (1 + 7 + 2 + 9) also add up to 19.
- The number 1729 is also the product of two prime numbers, 91 x 19.
- To spice things up even more, the 1729th prime number is 14759, and its mirror number, 95741, is also perfectly divisible by 19.
- The **7 Line Numbers** appended and written in reverse order form a number, **7654321**, which is a perfect multiple of 19. *Refer to the Table showing Chapter 1.*

Relation to Chapter 107

Furthermore, in the Quran, there are only 2 Chapters that have 7 verses, Chapter 1 and Chapter 107. The Chapter numbers appended (1107) and written in reverse order form a number **7011**, divisible by 19. The Chapter numbers (1, 107), along with their common verse count (7), form the number **11077**, which is again divisible by 19. One more key point is that there are only 7 Chapters after Chapter 107 in the Quran.

Intriguing pattern

An unexpected mathematical symmetry appears when the chapter's 7 lines are arranged in columns. The first three columns contain **31** letters each, forming a consistent and uniform pattern. *(Refer to Table 13.2)* However, as we move to the fourth column, it has **25** letters, which also matches the last 5 words in the last line segment, containing 25 letters. Notably, the connection between the 31 letters to these 50 letters and the Golden Ratio emerges, as multiplying 31 by 1.618 gives **50**. Moreover, dividing 31 by the Golden Ratio of 1.618 results in **19**, a significantly important number in Chapter 1, where verses 1, 5, 6, and part of verse 7 are all composed of exactly 19 letters.

Chapter 1 - Column Wise Distribution					
Last Line	**Line No.**	**4th Word**	**3rd Word**	**2nd Word**	**1st Word**
Last Part	1	ٱلرَّحِيمِ	الرَّحْمَـٰنِ	اللَّهِ	بِسْمِ
	2	الْعَالَمِينَ	رَبِّ	لِلَّهِ	الحَمدُ
غَيْرِ	3			الرَّحِيمِ	الرَّحمٰنِ
الْمَغْضُوبِ	4		الدِّينِ	يَومِ	مالِكِ
عَلَيْهِمْ	5	نَسْتَعِينُ	وَإِيَّاكَ	نَعبُدُ	إِيَّاكَ
وَلَا	6		الْمُستَقِيمَ	الصِّرَاطَ	اهدِنَا
الضَّالِّينَ	7	عَلَيْهِمْ	أَنْعَمْتَ	الَّذِينَ	صِرَاطَ
25	**LETTERS**	**25**	**31**	**31**	**31**

Table 13.2

With its intricate numerical structure, *Al-Fateha* demonstrates that the Quran's challenge is not merely rhetorical. The mathematical precision in every letter and word point to a sophistication beyond the human capacity to replicate or fully comprehend.

* * *

The Challenge of Chapter 108: *Al-Kausar* (The Abundance)

"The more passion we have to keep exploring, the more adventure awaits us." The smaller the chapter, the bigger the challenge. Chapter 108, *Al-Kausar,* stands as a leading example of this, consisting of just three lines. Despite its brevity, the numbers 10 and 7 prominently influence its structure. The dominance of the number 10 and the chapter's focus on "sacrifice" in the second line interestingly coincides with significant Islamic dates associated with sacrifice, such as the 10th of *Zilhajj* and the 10th of *Muharram*. In this chapter also the *dagger alif* has been replaced, and the original letters in the words أَعْطَيْنَاكَ and شَانِيَكَ as seen in early manuscripts of the Quran, have been restored.

Chapter - 108 - Al Kausar			
بِسْمِ ٱللَّهِ ٱلرَّحْمَـٰنِ ٱلرَّحِيمِ	Lines	Letters	Words
إِنَّا أَعْطَيْنَاكَ الْكَوْثَرَ ۝	1	16	3
فَصَلِّ لِرَبِّكَ وَانْحَرْ ۝	2	12	3
إِنَّ شَانِيَكَ هُوَ الْأَبْتَرُ ۝	3	15	4
TOTAL:	3	43	10

Quran: Chapter 108

Chapter Composition:

- The chapter consists of 3 lines.
- There are 43 letters in the chapter.
- The chapter is made up of 17 different letters.
- The chapter contains 10 words.

The Dominance of the Number 10

▪ The chapter has 10 letters without dots	ا ح ر ص ط ع ك ل ه و
▪ The 1st line is composed from10 letters.	ا ث ر ط ع ك ل ن و ي

▪ The 2nd line is composed from 10 letters.	ا ب ح ر ص ف ك ل ن و
▪ The 3rd line contains 10 dots.	ب ت ش ن ن ي
▪ The first letter of the chapter, أ *(Alif)*	repeats **10** times

The letter "ر" (R):

- The last letter of each line is "ر" (R)
- "ر" (R) is the 10th letter of the Arabic alphabet.
- If the letter positions of "ر" - 16th, 21st, 28th, 43rd, are added, they total 108, which is also the chapter number **(108)**.
- There are exactly 10 chapters in the Quran that end with the letter "ر" *(Refer to Table 13.3)*

10 Chapters that end with the letter "ر" (R)											
	1	*2*	*3*	*4*	*5*	*6*	*7*	*8*	*9*	***10***	Total
Chapter No.	5	22	31	42	54	60	97	100	103	108	**622**
Verses	120	78	34	53	55	13	5	11	3	3	**375**
Difference between Chapter No. and Verses (÷ 19)											**247**

Table 13.3

The difference between the sum of the Chapter numbers (622) and Verses (375) of these 10 chapters is **247**, which is an exact multiple of the distinguished number 19.

Repeated Letters:

- There are 6 letters (ا ر ك ل ن و) that appear in every line. So, all three lines have these 6 letters. The order of these letters corresponds to the 1st, 10th, 22nd, 23rd, 25th, and 27th letters of the Arabic alphabet. Adding these position numbers also results in **108**, which is the chapter number (108).

Center Letter "ب" (B)*:*

- The center of the chapter is the letter "ب", which is the 22nd letter, dividing the chapter into 21 letters before and 21 letters after it.
- The letter "ب" (B) occurs only twice in the chapter as the 22nd and 41st letters.
- The difference in the positions (41 - 22) of the letter "ب" is **19**.

Trail to 19:

- Appending the chapter number (108) with the number of lines (3) forms **1083**, divisible by 19.
- The number of letters in each line (16, 12, 15) when appended becomes **161215**, divisible by 19. Even the sum of their mirror numbers (61 + 21 + 51) totals **133**, also divisible by 19.
- The number of letters of each line written in column form **111625,** which is divisible by 19

The Dominance of the Number 7

▪ The chapter has 7 letters with dots	ب ت ث ش ف ن ي
▪ The first line has 7 unique letters	ث ر ط ع ل و ي
▪ The first line has 7 dots	ث ن ن ي

- The chapter is composed of **17** distinct letters of the Arabic language, and 17 is the 7th prime number.
- The center letter **"ب"** of the chapter divides the chapter into a multiple of 7, that is, **21** letters before and after it.
- The digits in the total number of letters (43) add up to 7 (4 + 3), and the number **43** is the 14th prime number, a multiple of 7.
- Appending the number of lines (3) with the number of letters (43) forms **343**, expressed as (7 x 7 x 7), the cube of 7.

- The placement of Chapter 108 when counted backwards (from the 114th chapter) is the 7th chapter.

The intricate and profound mathematical structure embedded within the shortest chapters of the Quran, such as Al-Kausar, underscores the divine nature of its composition. The perfect harmony of numbers and letters reveals an underlying complexity that defies human replication, reaffirming the Quran's challenge as a miraculous text beyond human capability and compilation.

* * *

The Challenge of Chapter 110: *Al-Nasr* (The Support)

In our search to unravel the mathematical marvels woven into the Quran, we have repeatedly seen that the smaller the chapter, the deeper the mathematics and the greater the challenge. Taking another step forward, we explore yet another chapter that exemplifies this principle.

Chapter 110, *Al-Nasr,* was the last revelation to Prophet Muhammed (S). This chapter, though brief, is steeped in the influence of prime numbers. All unique whole numbers that can only be divided by themselves and 1 are called prime numbers. This chapter stands as a mathematical masterpiece in its own right, highlighting the simplicity and singularity of prime numbers.

Chapter - 110 - Al Nasr			
بِسْمِ ٱللَّهِ ٱلرَّحْمَـٰنِ ٱلرَّحِيمِ	Lines	Letters	Words
إِذَا جَآءَ نَصْرُ اللَّهِ وَالْفَتْحُ ۞	1	18	5
وَرَأَيْتَ النَّاسَ يَدْخُلُونَ فِي دِينِ اللَّهِ أَفْوَاجًا ۞	2	31	7
فَسَبِّحْ بِحَمْدِ رَبِّكَ وَاسْتَغْفِرْهُ إِنَّهُ كَانَ تَوَّابًا ۞	3	30	7
TOTAL:	**3**	**79**	**19**

Quran: Chapter 110

Chapter Composition:

- The chapter consists of 3 lines.
- There are 79 letters in the chapter.
- The chapter consists of 20 different letters.
- The chapter contains **19** words.

Prime Numbers

- The chapter *Al-Nasr* has **3** lines, a prime number.
- The total number of letters is **79**, also a prime number.
- The chapter contains **19** words, yet another prime number.
- The unique letters (خ ذ ص غ م) in the chapter are **5**, a prime number.
- The number of words in each line is 5, 7, and 7 — all prime numbers. When these numbers are appended, they form **577**, which is itself a prime number.

The mathematical elegance of prime numbers doesn't stop there. The chapter continues to reveal its hidden numerical harmony:

- Combining the number of letters (18) and words (5) in the first line gives us 185. Combining the chapter number (110) and the number of lines (3) gives us the 185th prime number — **1103**.
- Appending the 31 letters and 7 words in the second line forms **317**, another prime number.
- Appending the 30 letters and 7 words in the third line yields **307**, which is also a prime number.

The chapter's very structure and its relationship with prime numbers are even more compelling:

- The difference between the chapter number (110) and the number of letters (79) is **31**, a prime number.

- The difference between the chapter number (110) and the number of lines (3) is **107**, a prime number.
- The sum of the chapter number (110) and the number of lines (3) is **113**, another prime number.

The chapter *Al-Nasr* also maintains a mathematical balance in the letters that appear throughout:

- The number of letters (ا ت ر ف ن ه و) that appear in all three lines is 7, a prime number.
- If we add the unique letters in each line, that is,10 in the first, 6 in the second, and 3 in the third line, the total is **19**, another prime number. *Refer to Table 13.4*

Unique Letters - Prime Number		
Line No.	Unique Letters	Total
1	ت ج ح ذ ر ص ف ن ه و	10
2	ت ج خ ر س ه	6
3	د غ م	3
	Total:	19

Table 13.4

Center Letter Alif أ

- The chapter begins with the letter *Alif* أ
- The chapter ends with the letter *Alif* أ
- The center of the chapter is also the letter *Alif* أ
- The total number of *Alif* in the chapter is **17**, a Prime number
- Interestingly, the center *Alif* of the chapter is also the center *Alif* of all 17 *Alifs,* dividing them equally, with 8 *Alifs* before and 8 *Alifs* after the center *Alif.*

The Challenge of Chapter 97: *Al-Qadr* (Power)

In the vast collection of divine revelations, a small chapter, Al-Qadr, composed of only five lines, lies packed with a message so immense that it demands attention from both the seeker of faith and the admirer of logic.

Chapter 97 - Qadr (Power)			
بِسْمِ ٱللَّهِ ٱلرَّحْمَـٰنِ ٱلرَّحِيمِ	Lines	Letters	Words
إِنَّا أَنْزَلْنَاهُ فِي لَيْلَةِ الْقَدْرِ	1	21	5
وَمَا أَدْرَاكَ مَا لَيْلَةُ الْقَدْرِ	2	19	5
لَيْلَةُ ٱلْقَدْرِ خَيْرٌ مِّنْ أَلْفِ شَهْرٍ	3	20	6
تَنَزَّلُ الْمَلَائِكَةُ وَٱلرُّوحُ فِيهَا بِإِذْنِ رَبِّهِم مِّن كُلِّ أَمْرٍ	4	37	9
سَلَـٰمٌ هِيَ حَتَّىٰ مَطْلَعِ ٱلْفَجْرِ	5	17	5
TOTAL :	**5**	**114**	**30**

Quran: Chapter 97

Surah Al-Qadr, Chapter 97 of the Qur'an. A chapter revealed not just on a momentous night, but about the very night itself, a night known as *Lailatul Qadr,* the Night of Power, the night when the Quran was first revealed to Prophet Muhammed (S). This night, hidden in the final ten nights of Ramadan, is described by the Qur'an as "better than a thousand months." A single night of immense power. But here's the mystery: which night is it?

Traditions tell us that the Night of Qadr falls on one of the five odd nights of the last ten days of Ramadan: the 21st, 23rd, 25th, 27th, or 29th. But what if the chapter revealed about this night also contains the key to unlock it? Could mathematics, with its elegant order, point us to one of these sacred nights as the Night of Qadr?

Can Numbers Reveal the Night?

Strangely enough, when these five odd night numbers are stitched together (21, 23, 25, 27, 29), they form different sequences. One of the sequences, 212325, is perfectly divisible by 19. Even narrowing in on the middle two, 2527, we again find a number divisible by 19. Is this a coincidence? Or simply Mathematics glowing in the dark, showing the way like a lighthouse in the vast ocean.

Let's look into the structure of this chapter, using mathematics as our guide and numbers as our light.

Chapter Composition:

- The chapter *Al-Qadr* consists of 5 lines.
- There are 114 letters in the chapter.
- The chapter contains 30 words.

Chapter Placement:

- The Chapter before 97, Chapter 96, has **19** verses
- The Chapter after 97, Chapter 98, has 8 verses, and **988** is divisible by 19.

Anchored by 19 and 23

- The chapter consists of **23** different letters.
- 5 Letters are omitted in the chapter (ث ص ض ظ غ). The alphabetical positions of these Arabic letters (4, 14, 15, 17, 19) sum up to **69**, a number divisible by 23.
- The difference between Chapter Number 97 and its total number of Verses 5 is (97 - 5), which equals **92**, and is divisible by 23.

- The chapter *Al-Qadr* has **114** letters, a number divisible by 19 and also matching the total number of chapters revealed in the Quran.
- The chapter *Al-Qadr has* a total number of **30** words, 30 being the 19th composite number.
- Counting backwards, the **19th** word of the Chapter is *Al-Qadr,* which is also the name of the Chapter.
- The first letter of the chapter and the Arabic Alphabet, أ *"Alif",* appears **19** times in the chapter.
- The 23rd letter of the Arabic Alphabet, ل also appears **19** times.
- The frequency of the 23rd letter, ل in Lines 1 to 5 forms a sequence 4, 3, 4, 5, 3, when appended forms the number **43453**, perfectly divisible by 19.
- The 10th letter of the Arabic Alphabet, ر appears **10** times.
- Counted backwards, ر is the **19th** letter of the Arabic alphabet.
- The occurrence of letter, ر in Lines 1 to 5 forms a sequence 1, 2, 3, 3, 1, when appended forms the number **12331**, perfectly divisible by 19.
- In sequence, when appended, Verse numbers 2, 3, and Verse numbers 3,4,5 give the numbers **23** and **345**, which are both divisible by 23, whereas the mirror of Verse numbers 1 to 5 is **54321**, which is divisible by 19.

Footprints of 23

- The phrase *Lailatul Qadr* begins with the letter ل - the 23rd letter of the Arabic alphabet. Additionally, ل is uniquely emphasized by appearing thrice in the phrase *Lailatul Qadr* (**لَيْلَةِ ٱلْقَدْرِ**), where the phrase itself is repeated thrice in the chapter. So, in all, there are 9 ل in all the instances of *Lailatul Qadr,* and the 9th Prime number is **23**.

- The center line, which is line number 3, has 20 letters. When added (3 + 20), we get **23**.
- The 23rd word of the chapter *Al-Qadr* is **من**
- The 23rd letter of the chapter is **م** *(Meem)*, and counting backwards, the 23rd letter of the chapter is **ن** *(Noon)*.
- The total number of **م** *(Meem)* and **ن** *(Noon)* in the chapter is 9 and 7, respectively. The appended sequence forms **97**, pointing back to the chapter number 97
- The word **من** appears twice, it is the 53rd and 54th as well as the 91st & 92nd letter of the chapter. When these numbers are placed in sequence, **5453** and **9291**, they are both divisible by 19.
- The 23rd word of the chapter, counting backwards, is **ما** which is the 1st and 24th letter of the Arabic Alphabet. The difference between their count (24 -1) equals **23**.
- The number of Letters in Lines 1 to 5, stitched together, is 2119203717, divisible by **97**, which is the chapter number, whereas its mirror number, which is **7173029112**, is divisible by 19.
- The number of Words in Lines 1 to 5, appended, is **55695**. Its mirror number, 59655, is also divisible by **97**, which is the chapter number.

Shadows of 23

All 5 lines contain letters that are repeated 2 and 3 times. Four of these lines have consecutive Arabic alphabet letters repeated 2 and 3 times.

- 1st Line, letters **ن هـ** are repeated **2, 3** times
- 2nd Line, letters **ل م** are repeated **2, 3** times
- 3rd Line, letters **ر ي** are repeated **2, 3** times
- 4th Line, letters **هـ و** are repeated **2, 3** times
- 5th Line, letters **ل م** are repeated **2, 3** times

Total In Chapter	Letter	Line No.	Total In Line
10	ر	Line 2	**2**
		Line 3	**3**
9	ه	Line 3	**2**
		Line 4	**3**
19			

Table 13.5

- Two letters, ر and ه, which are the last letters of the words *Lailah* and *Al-Qadr*, occur 2 and 3 times consecutively in line numbers 2, 3, and 3, 4, respectively. Appending line numbers, we get 23 and 34, the sum of which is **57**, a multiple of 19. *Refer to Table 13.5*
- Letter ر appears 10 times in the chapter, and letter ه appears 9 times throughout the chapter, both adding to **19**.

Echoes of 23 in words

- The word *"Qadr"* (Power) appears 4 times in the Quran, specifically in 2 Chapters, Chapter Numbers 77 and 97. It appears in 77:23, 97:1, 97:2, and 97:3. From the first occurrence of *"Qadr"* in Chapter 77 to the next occurrence in Chapter 97, there are **19** chapters. If we append the chapter numbers to form **7797**, we get a number that is a perfect multiple of 23.
- Interestingly, the first occurrence of the word *Qadr* is in Chapter 77 at verse 23, while in Chapter 97, it appears in verses 2 and 3, again hinting at the number 23. The sum of the chapter numbers (77 + 97 + 97 + 97) equals **368**, a perfect multiple of 23, and its first digits combined give **7999**, which is divisible by 19. The verse numbers (23, 1, 2, 3) combined give **23123**, a perfect multiple of 19.

- The letters making up the word *"Qadr"* (ق د ر) in the Arabic alphabet are located in the 21st, 8th, and 10th positions. Operating (21 + 8 - 10), we arrive at the sign and the seal, the number 19.
- The word *"Nazalna"* (We have sent/revealed) appears 6 times in the Quran. Its First occurrence is at 2:23, and its Last occurrence is at 76:23. Both occurrences of the word "*Nazalna*" are anchored by verse number 23.
- The difference between the last occurrence of the word *"Nazalna"*, which is at 76:23, and the total number of verses in the Quran, which is 6236, gives (7623 - 6236). The calculation results in **1387**, which is divisible by 19.
- The 2-word phrase, *"Inna Anzalnaho"*, appears 3 times in the Quran. In addition to Chapter 97:1, it is also found in Chapter 12:2 and Chapter 44:3. These two verses, 2 and 3, when combined, hint at the number 23. When we add math operators to these occurrences (971 + 443 - 122), we get **1292** - divisible by 19.
- The word *"Anzalna"* without any suffix appears first time at 2:99, and **299** is a perfect multiple of 23. Its last occurrence is at 64:8, and the combined numbers are **648299**, which is divisible by 19.
- The first mention of the word *"Quran"* and the month of *"Ramadhan"*, along with the word *"Unzala"* (revealed), is in 2:185. The number 2185 is perfectly divisible by 19 and 23, and can also be expressed as a product of 95 and 23.
- The word *"Unzala"* itself appears 95 times in the Quran, and 95 is a perfect multiple of 19. The first occurrence of *"Unzala"* is in verse 2:24, and its last occurrence is in verse 65:10. The difference between 6510 and 224 is **6486**, which is again divisible by 23.
- The 2-word phrase *"Lailat-ul-Qadr"* appears exactly 3 times in verses 97:1, 97:2, 97:3. The verse numbers contain the number 23. Appending only the verse numbers with the chapter number, we

get 12397, which is divisible by 23, whereas adding the chapter number thrice as it appears and subtracting the verse numbers (97-1) + (97-2) + (97-3) from it, equals **285**, perfectly divisible by 19.

- The phrase *"Lailat-ul-Qadr"* has a total of 9 letters. Interestingly, the 9th prime number is **23**.

The numbers 19 and 23 keep reappearing, like divine markers stitched into the very fabric of *Surah Al-Qadr*. Their recurrence is not subtle; it is deliberate, persistent, and mathematically elegant. If there is a language beyond words in the Qur'an, it is numbers, and here, they speak clearly. Amidst the mystery surrounding the exact identity of the Night of Power, mathematics seems to pierce through the historical veils of ambiguity. If history has concealed, then mathematics has revealed, with clarity, logic, and perfection. If there is any night that the numbers seem to crown, it is the 23rd night. Whether as a date or a signature, the number 23 resounds in this chapter like a bell struck by the unseen, which is loud, precise, and profoundly intentional.

How more eloquently must the Quran offer perfect mathematics within its poetry to prove its divine composition or deny history the chance to raise doubts about its alteration? A remarkable demonstration of the Quran's mathematical harmony can be seen within its briefest chapters.

This book serves as an eye-opener, offering a glimpse into the remarkable mathematical intricacies within the small chapters of the Quran. There are many more examples and numerous chapters whose mathematical patterns are truly mind-boggling. However, keeping it concise, it is sufficient to grasp the underlying theory of mathematics in the Quran.

14

THE MYSTERY LETTERS - THE MUQATTAAT

The clash intensifies as Mathematics, relentless and unwavering, showcases the universal language of numbers in a sacred text, making it impossible to produce. History, once a towering figure of authority, now stumbles under the weight of Mathematics. Numbers do not mislead, and patterns do not lie. The balance shifts, and History finds itself on the losing side, while the outcome leans toward the unwavering logic and magic of Mathematics.

In the chapters of the Quran, there exists an area shrouded in mystery, the domain of *Al-Hurouf Al-Muqattaat*, the enigmatic letters that adorn the beginnings of 29 chapters. As we stand on the threshold of this uncharted territory, armed with the tools of mathematics and the Arabic Alphabet, we embark on a quest to unravel the secrets concealed within these cryptic symbols.

13 أ	7 ح	6 ر	5 س	3 ص	4 ط	2 ع
2 ق	1 ك	13 ل	17 م	1 ن	2 هـ	2 ي

Table 14.1: Al Hurouf Al-Muqattaat and their Count (78)

Al Hurouf Al-Muqattaat

Also known as the Separated Letters or the Mysterious Letters, *Al Hurouf Al-Muqattaat* are a set of letters that appear at the beginning of 29 Chapters of the Quran. In total, there are 30 *Muqattaat* distributed in 29 Chapters. Chapter 42 is exceptional because it has 2 *Muqattaat* written in 2 verses, read in continuation, and referred to as 1 unique pattern. The 30 *Muqattaat* add up to **78** letters, made up of a combination of **14** letters. Although the meaning and significance of these separated letters remain unknown, Mathematics could provide some insight into their mysterious arrangements. *Refer to Table 14.1,* which shows the 14 letters and the number of times they have been used in the Quran in forming the *Muqattaat* patterns. The 14 letters form 14 different patterns. The 14 different patterns, without repetitions, add up to 38 letters, a multiple of 19. *(Refer to Table 14.2)*

14 Different Patterns of Muqattat													
9									5				
ن	ق	حم عسق	حم	ص	يس	طس	طسم	طه	كهيعص	المر	الر	المص	الم
1	1	5	2	1	2	2	3	2	5	4	3	4	3
19									19				
Total Letters of 14 different patterns = 38 Letters (19 + 19)													

Table 14.2

Examining the chart displaying the *Muqattaat* pattern in chronological order as they appear in the Quran, we notice a distinct division. Dividing it into two sets, each comprising exactly **19** letters, allows us to uncover further insights. In the first set of 19 letters, there is a precise symmetry, a combination of 9 different letters forming 5 patterns. As we move to the next set of 19 letters, we encounter a total of 9 patterns, composed of 10 different letters. After analysing both sets, number **19** from 9 and 10 different letters, and from 9 and 5 patterns, the number **95**, a multiple of 19, is implicitly visible.

MUQATAAT IN THE QURAN

S.No.	Name	MUQATAAT IN SERIES		Chp. No.	Verses	Chp. Gap
#1	Al-Baqara	الم	REPEAT (1)	2	286	
#2	Aal-E-Imran	الم	REPEAT (2)	3	200	3
#3	Al-A'raf	**المص**	**UNQ (1)**	7	206	2
#4	Yunus	الر	REPEAT (3)	10	109	
#5	Hud	الر	REPEAT (4)	11	123	
#6	Yusuf	الر	REPEAT (5)	12	111	
#7	Ar-Ra'd	**المر**	**UNQ (2)**	13	43	
#8	Ibrahim	الر	REPEAT (6)	14	52	
#9	Al-Hijr	الر	REPEAT (7)	15	99	3
#10	Maryam	**كهيعص**	**UNQ (3)**	19	98	
#11	Ta-Ha	**طه**	**UNQ (4)**	20	135	5
#12	Ash-Shu'ara	طسم	REPEAT (8)	26	227	
#13	An-Naml	**طس**	**UNQ (5)**	27	93	
#14	Al-Qasas	طسم	REPEAT (9)	28	88	
#15	**Al-Ankabut**	**الم**		**29**	**69**	**MID**
#16	Ar-Rum	الم	REPEAT (1)	30	60	
#17	Luqman	الم	REPEAT (2)	31	34	
#18	As-Sajda	الم	REPEAT (3)	32	30	3
#19	Ya Sin	**يس**	**UNQ (1)**	36	83	1
#20	Saad	**ص**	**UNQ (2)**	38	88	1
#21	Al Mu'min	حم	REPEAT (4)	40	85	
#22	Fussilat	حم	REPEAT (5)	41	54	
#23 #24	Ash-Shura	**حم** **عسق**	**UNQ (3)**	42	53	
#25	Az-Zukhruf	حم	REPEAT (6)	43	89	
#26	Ad-Dukhan	حم	REPEAT (7)	44	59	
#27	Al-Jathiya	حم	REPEAT (8)	45	37	
#28	Al-Ahqaf	حم	REPEAT (9)	46	35	3
#29	Qaf	**ق**	**UNQ (4)**	50	45	17
#30	Al-Qalam	**ن**	**UNQ (5)**	68	52	

3
2
3
5
3
1
1
3
17

Σ = 38

Table 14-A

MUQATAAT SORTED					
S.No.	Name	MUQATAAT REPEAT / UNIQUE		Chp. No.	Verses
#1	Al-Baqara	الم	REPEAT (1)	2	286
#2	Al-i-Imran	الم	REPEAT (2)	3	200
#3	Yunus	الر	REPEAT (3)	10	109
#4	Hud	الر	REPEAT (4)	11	123
#5	Yusuf	الر	REPEAT (5)	12	111
#6	Ibrahim	الر	REPEAT (6)	14	52
#7	Al-Hijr	الر	REPEAT (7)	15	99
#8	Ash-Shu'ara	طسم	REPEAT (8)	26	227
#9	Al-Qasas	طسم	REPEAT (9)	28	88
#10	Al-Ankabut	الم	REPEAT (10)	29	69
#11	Ar-Rum	الم	REPEAT (11)	30	60
#12	Luqman	الم	REPEAT (12)	31	34
#13	As-Sajda	الم	REPEAT (13)	32	30
#14	Al Mu'min	حم	REPEAT (14)	40	85
#15	Fussilat	حم	REPEAT (15)	41	54
#16	Az-Zukhruf	حم	REPEAT (16)	43	89
#17	Ad-Dukhan	حم	REPEAT (17)	44	59
#18	Al-Jathiya	حم	REPEAT (18)	45	37
#19	Al-Ahqaf	حم	REPEAT (19)	46	35

#1	Al-A'raf	**المص**	**UNIQE (1)**	7	206
#2	Ar-Ra'd	**المر**	**UNIQE (2)**	13	43
#3	Maryam	**كهيعص**	**UNIQE (3)**	19	98
#4	Ta-Ha	**طه**	**UNIQE (4)**	20	135
#5	An-Naml	**طس**	**UNIQE (5)**	27	93
#6	Ya Sin	**يس**	**UNIQE (6)**	36	83
#7	Saad	**ص**	**UNIQE (7)**	38	88
#8	Ash-Shura	**حم** **عسق**	**UNIQE (8)**	42	53
#9	Qaf	**ق**	**UNIQE (9)**	50	45
#10	Al-Qalam	**ن**	**UNIQE (10)**	68	52

Table 14-B

The analysis of the *Muqattaat*, the mysterious letters appearing in the Quran, reveals a fascinating correlation between their arrangement and numerical patterns. *(Refer to Table 14-A and 14-B)*

The 29 chapters that contain Muqattaat are: [2, 3, 7, 10, 11, 12, 13, 14, 15, 19, 20, 26, 27, 28, 29, 30, 31, 32, 36, 38, 40, 41, 42, 43, 44, 46, 50, 68]. There are exactly 19 chapters from Chapter 50 to 68.

Interestingly, there are exactly 29 chapters in the Quran that do not contain the word "Allah" الله in their text. They are: [54, 55, 56, 68, 75, 78, 80, 82, 83, 86, 89, 90, 92, 93, 94, 97, 99, 100, 101, 102, 103, 105, 106, 107, 108, 109, 111, 113, 114]. There is only one chapter that is common between them, Chapter 68. The 3 chapters preceding Chapter 68 are 56, 55, and 54. Incidentally, **565554** is perfectly divisible by 19.

The deliberate arrangement of the *Muqattaat* hints at a deeper significance beyond their surface appearance. It invites further exploration into the hidden links and pointers within these mysterious letters, guiding us on a journey of discovery into the heart of the Quran's sacred text.

Distribution of Muqattaat:

As we delve deeper into the enigmatic territory of the *Muqattaat*, their distribution across the Quran reveals a masterpiece of mathematical harmony that surpasses mere coincidence. *(Refer to Table 14-A and 14.3)*

Distribution of Muqataat	
First **10** Muqataat	: In First **19** Chapters *(Ch. 1 to 19)*
Next **10** Muqataat	: In Next **19** Chapters *(Ch. 20 to 38)*
Last **10** Muqataat	: In Next **30** Chapters *(Ch. 39 to 68)*

*(30 is the **19**th Composite Number)*

Table 14.3

The Quran presents the 30 *Muqattaat (Refer to Table 5.2 - Quran's structure),* divided into three distinct sets, each comprising 10 *Muqattaat.* The meticulous arrangement unfolds across the chapters:

- the first set of 10, gracing the initial 19 chapters *(Ch. 1 to 19)*,
- followed by the second set of 10, in the subsequent 19 chapters *(Ch. 20 to 38)*, and
- the final set adorning the remaining 30 chapters *(Ch. 39 to 68)*. The significance of the number 30 is that it is the 19th composite number.

The list of the first 19 composite numbers is given in *Table 14.4*

List of - 19 Composite Numbers										
	1st	2nd	3rd	4th	5th	6th	7th	8th	9th	10th
Composite	4	6	8	9	10	12	14	15	16	18
	11th	12th	13th	14th	15th	16th	17th	18th	**19th**	
Composite	20	21	22	24	25	26	27	28	**30**	

Table 14.4

Recurrence of the Letters of Muqattaat:

The count or frequency of the letters in *Al-Hurouf Al-Muqattaat* is intriguing in itself. Their occurrence, combined and written in sequence, sorted from the first letter of the Arabic alphabet (أ) to the last, results in **137653422-11317122**. *Refer to Table 14.1 for details.* The second part of this number, 11317122, is perfectly divisible by 19, and the mirror number of the first part, 224356731, is also a perfect multiple of 19.

In the Quran, from Chapter 2 to 68, some chapters with Muqattaat appear together with continuous chapter numbers, while others have gaps between them. Interestingly, the total of these gaps [3 + 2 + 3 + 5 + 3 + 1 + 1 + 1 + 3 + 17] adds up to **38**, a multiple of 19. *Refer to Table 14.1 for details.* Additionally, the number formed by combining the digits of the gaps, **3235311317**, is also perfectly divisible by 19.

Muqattaat Patterns

Within this complex maze of 14 patterns of *Muqattaat*, 10 unique patterns and 4 repeated patterns intertwine, forming the fabric of *Muqattaat*, the disconnected letters. *Refer to Table 14.5*

10 Unique Patterns

	ن	ق	حم عسق	ص	يس	طس	طه	كهيعص	المر	المص
Unique	1	1	1	1	1	1	1	1	1	1

4 Repeated Patterns

	حم	طسم	الر	الم
Repeated	6	2	5	6

Σ OF DIGITS = **19**

Table 14.5

- The 4 repeated patterns piece together (6 + 2 + 5 + 6) times, to form exactly 19 *Muqattaats.*
- The 10 unique patterns consist of 14 different letters, while the 4 repeated patterns consist of 7 different letters.
- When the 10 unique pattern numbers are multiplied (1x1x1x1x1x1x1x1x1x1) and the 4 repeated pattern numbers are multiplied (6x2x5x6), we get 1 and 360. When these two numbers are added, the result is **361**, which is equal to (19^2), the square of 19.

* * *

Upon closer examination, the mid-point of the distribution of *Muqattaat* unveils a captivating fact. As there are 30 *Muqattaat*, distributed in 29 chapters, the 15th *Muqattaat* is the midpoint and one of the important references. Incidentally, the 15th *Muqattaat is* precisely placed in Chapter **29**. *Refer to Table 14-A*

Remarkably, symmetry seeps into this sacred *Muqattaat*, with an equal distribution of unique and repeated *Muqattaat* chapters before and after the midpoint. Before and after Chapter 29, there is an **equal distribution** of 5 chapters of unique *Muqattaat. Refer to Table 14.6*

Before and After Chapter No. 29 - Unique Muqattat						
	Ch. 7	Ch. 13	Ch. 19	Ch. 20	Ch. 27	
Before Ch. 29	المص	المر	كهيعص	طه	طس	***5** Unique Muqattat*
Chapter 29						
	Ch. 36	Ch. 38	Ch. 42	Ch. 50	Ch. 68	
After Ch. 29	يس	ص	حم عسق	ق	ن	***5** Unique Muqattat*

Table 14.6

Similarly, before and after Chapter 29, there is an **equal distribution** of 9 chapters of repeated *Muqattaat. Refer to Table 14.7*

Before and After Chapter No. 29 - Repeated Muqattat						
	Ch. 2	Ch. 3	Ch. 10	Ch. 11	Ch. 12	
Before Ch. 29	الم	الم	الر	الر	الر	***9** Repeat Muqattat*
	Ch. 14	Ch. 15	Ch. 26	Ch. 28		
	الر	الر	طسم	طسم		
Chapter 29						
	Ch. 30	Ch. 31	Ch. 32	Ch. 40	Ch. 41	
After Ch. 29	الم	الم	الم	حم	حم	***9** Repeat Muqattat*
	Ch. 43	Ch. 44	Ch. 45	Ch. 46		
	حم	حم	حم	حم		

Table 14.7

So, the entire Quran has Unique *Muqattaat* and Repeated *Muqattaat*, equally distributed, before and after Chapter 29.

* * *

Furthermore, the numerical significance extends beyond mere distribution. There are 19 *Muqattaat* in the Quran, which are written as a separate verse having a distinct verse number. Additionally, there are 11 *Muqattaat* that are attached to the first verse at the start of the chapter and are therefore not given a separate identity or verse number. Even though these 11 *Muqattaat* are a connected part of the first verse, they are still considered a separate entity. *Refer to Table 14.8*

Muqataat - Separate Verse Number		
	Chapter Nos.	
19 Separate - Muqataat	2, 3, 7, **19**, 20, 26, 28, 29, 30, 31, 32, 40, 41, 42, 42, 43, 44, 45, 46	Σ = **570** *(19 x 30)*

Muqataat - Joint to the 1st Verse		
	Chapter Nos.	
11 Joint - Muqataat	10, 11, 12, 13, 14, 15, 27, 36, **38**, 50, 68	

Table 14.8

Amazingly, the sum of all the 19-chapter numbers where the *Muqattaat* are written as separate verses is **570**. The number 570 resonates as a multiple of 19, expressed as 19 x 30. The significance of the number 30 is that it is the 19th composite number.

In both cases, whether the *Muqattaat* are treated as a separate verse or as part of the first verse, the chapter numbers that are multiples of 19 are present in equal measure (1:1). In the 19th chapter, the Muqattaat are a separate verse, while in the 38th chapter, they are incorporated as part of the first verse.

Delving deeper into the composition of the *Muqattaat*, the presence of unique and repeated letters unveils another layer of divine precision. Out of the 14 letters of *Muqattaat*, 2 stand as solitary entities, used only once, while the remaining 12 combine and mix to form a total of **76** letters. The number 76 is a multiple of 19, expressed as 19 x 4.

Unique Letters	Repeated Letters
2 Letters - ك ن	**76** Letters *(19 x 4)*

***

Next, let us scrutinize three consecutive chapters, Chapter 26, Chapter 27, and Chapter 28, all commencing with "طس" and perceive that the very fabric of the Quran's composition is woven with threads of divine precision. These cryptic beginnings serve as a clarion call to unravel the mathematical mysteries concealed within the Quran's sacred verses.

The Mystery of Chapter 26 - طسم

In the vast ocean of the Quran, Chapter 26 stands as a testament to the meticulous design infused within every verse. Chapter 26 opens with the enigmatic *Muqattaat* ["طسم ۝"], a separate verse with a distinct verse number. Diving into the numerical fabric of Chapter 26, we encounter remarkable patterns that defy mere coincidence.

- With a total of 227 verses, the mirror number of **722**, which is a multiple of 19.
- The center of the chapter is Verse **114**, which is a multiple of 19, and this 114th verse has exactly 19 letters.
- A fascinating observation emerges when considering the distribution of the letter "م" within the chapter. The difference

between the Chapter Number and its total verses (227 – 26) is **201**. Interestingly, out of its 227 verses, 201 contain the letter "م" while the remaining 26 verses do not. *Refer to Table 14.9*

Distribution of - Letter "م"		
Chapter No.	Verses	Difference
26	227	(227 – 26) = **201**
Verses Without "م"		Verses With "م"
26		**201**

Table 14.9

- The 26 verses of Chapter No. 26, without the letter "م" are:

12	13	33	46	59	74	78	84	108	110	126	128	131
134	137	144	147	150	**152**	163	171	179	196	204	214	219

- The 19th time a verse without the letter "م" appears is in Verse **152**, which again is a multiple of 19.
- The *Muqattaat*, comprising 14 letters, are repeated to build 78 letters (26 x 3), holds a secret code of significance. Let us count the occurrences of letters ط س م within the *Muqattaat*. The entire list of *Muqattaat* contains **4** "ط", **5** "س", and **17** "م". These letters (4 + 5 + 17) add up to 26, echoing the chapter number. The occurrences can be referred to in *Tables 14.1 and 14.10*

Occurences in Muqattat		
ط	س	م
4	5	17

(4 + 5 + 17) = **26**

Table 14.10

- The placement order of these letters م س ط in the *Hija'i* Arabic Alphabet further illuminates the divine harmony woven into Chapter 26. The letter "ط" is the **16th** letter, "س" is the **12th** letter, and "م" is the **24th** letter. The cumulative sum of their placement order (16 + 12 + 24) equals **52**, twice the chapter number 26.

Hijaai Arabic Count		
ط	س	م
16th Letter	12th Letter	24th Letter

(16 + 12 + 24) = 52 = (**26** x 2)

Table 14.11

- To add another layer to the enigma, in Chapter 26 of the Quran, there are 227 verses. Among these 227 verses, other than the 1st verse, which is the *Muqattaat*, 9 verses contain all three letters of the *Muqattaat* (م س ط), while 11 verses contain none of the three letters. This gives a total of **21** verses (1 + 9 + 11) that include or exclude all 3 letters of the *Muqattaat*. Interestingly, the number 227 is the 49th Prime Number, and all the verse numbers that are in multiples of 49 are a part of one of these 21 verses, whether through the presence or complete absence of all three *Muqattaat* letters. *Refer to Table 14.12*

طسم in Multiples of 49		
	Verse No.	طسم
(49 x 1)	Vs. **49**	Has all the 3 letters طسم
(49 x 2)	(Uptill) Vs. **98**	Sum of all طسم = 260 (÷ 26)
(49 x 3)	Vs. **147**	Has none of the 3 letters طسم
(49 x 4)	Vs. **196**	Has none of the 3 letters طسم

Table 14.12

- After the first verse, all three (3) letters of the *Muqattaat* (طسم) appear together for the first time in Verse **49** (49 x 1). Verse 49 also has the maximum letters of the *Muqattaat* in the Chapter, totaling 15.
- Additionally, from Verse 1 to Verse **98** (49 x 2), the cumulative total of these 3 letters of *Muqattaat* is exactly 260, a number divisible by the chapter number 26.
- Whereas verse **147** (49 x 3) and verse **196** (49 x 4), both multiples of 49, do not have any of the 3 letters of *Muqattaat.*

The Word "Rasool" **رَسُول** *(Messenger)*

In the Quran, words often carry a deeper numerical importance, highlighting the precision and balance within the sacred text. One such example is the word *"Rasool"*, without its variations.

- The word *"Rasool"* is mentioned exactly **52** times throughout the Quran. Interestingly, 52 is a multiple of 26, and the central point of the number 52 is also 26. The 26th instance of the word *"Rasool"* directly connects to the 26th chapter of the Quran, specifically in verse 26:107, positioning it at the heart of this numerical symmetry.
- In verse **26:107**, the sum of the chapter number (26) and the verse number (107) equals **133**, a number divisible by 19. Furthermore, appending the numbers 26 and 107 forms **26107**, which is the 2869th prime number, and interestingly, 2869 is also divisible by 19.

These mathematical relationships in the Quran highlight the idea that its words are not placed randomly but follow a deliberate pattern.

The Word " Qaala" **قَال** *in Chapter 26*

Another example where a word carries a numerical resonance is the word *"Qaala"* (**قَال**) which marks the beginning of Verse 26 of Chapter

26 and appears precisely **26** times within the chapter. Each occurrence is a testament to the divine precision that underlies every aspect of the Quran's composition.

- The first word of Chapter 26: Verse 26 is *"Qaala"* قَالَ
- Total word count of *"Qaala"* **قَالَ** in the entire Chapter is 26 times

Within the verses of this chapter, we encounter another remarkable phenomenon - a series of precise gaps where the word *"Qaala"* **قَالَ** is absent. These gaps, in multiples of 19 verses, are a testament to the meticulous design of the Quran. *Refer to Table 14.13*

- From Verse 75 to Verse 112 (including both verses), there are **38** (19 x 2) verses devoid of the word *"Qaala"*.
- Again, from Verse 117 to Verse 155, there are **38** (19 x 2) verses in between where the word *"Qaala"* is absent.
- Also, from verse 168 to verse 188, there is a gap of exactly **19** verses without the word *"Qaala"*.
- Finally, from Verse 189 to the end of the chapter at Verse 227, there are again **38** verses with no occurrences of the word *"Qaala."*

"Qaala" قَالَ

Gaps in the Multiple of 19

Verses	No "Qaala" قَالَ
Vs. **75** -to- Vs. **112**	= 38 Verses (Both Inclusive)
Vs. **117** -to- Vs. **155**	= 38 Verses (19 x 2)
Vs. **168** -to- Vs. **188**	= 19 Verses (Gap)
Vs. **189** -to- Vs. **227**	= 38 Verses

Table 14.13

The intricate design of Chapter 26 and its compilation are no ordinary feat; it is a testament to the symphony of numbers, letters, and words that lie at the heart of the Quran's revelation.

* * *

The Mystery of Chapter 27 - طس

Chapter 27 of the Quran emerges as a powerful testament to the divine composition and compilation. Its mathematical intricacies are so powerful that this one chapter, warrior in our context, alone can challenge historical narrations and decisively prove the Quran's divine compilation. With its unique numerical patterns and structure, Chapter 27 is the ultimate weapon to confront and defeat the uncertainties posed by history. Its embedded mathematics speaks louder than historical accounts and has the potential to emerge victorious in the battle against time. This chapter commences with the unique *Muqattaat* طس attached to the first verse, seamlessly integrated into its divine composition.

Exploring the numerical harmony of Chapter 27, we discover profound patterns encoded within the numbers of its verses. With 93 verses, the chapter unfolds with a mathematical precision that illuminates its divine design. The digit 9, when multiplied by 3, reveals the chapter number- **27**. Furthermore, when we append the chapter number (27) to the total number of verses (93), we obtain **2793**, a number perfectly divisible by 19. Similarly, the mirrored form of these numbers, 7239, also yields a multiple of 19. *Refer to Table 14.14*

<table>
<tr><th>Chapter No.</th><th>Total Verses</th></tr>
<tr><td>27</td><td>93</td></tr>
<tr><td colspan="2">2793 is divisible by (÷ 19)</td></tr>
<tr><td colspan="2">Mirror of Both the Numbers</td></tr>
<tr><td>72</td><td>39</td></tr>
<tr><td colspan="2">7239 is divisible by (÷ 19)</td></tr>
<tr><td colspan="2">And (9 x 3) = 27 = Chapter Number</td></tr>
</table>

Table 14.14

Muqattaat Patterns

The *Muqattaat* of this chapter unveils astonishing mathematical symmetries.

- The divine precision is unmistakable with exactly **27** occurrences of the letter **ط** in the chapter, mirroring the chapter number (27), and precisely **93** occurrences of the letter **س** in the chapter, matching the total number of verses (93).
- Additionally, 13 verses contain both *Muqattaat* letters **ط** and **س**, while 26 verses do not contain **ط** and **س** together, resulting in a total of 39 distinct verses, which is the mirror of 93 - a reflection of the total verses (93) in the chapter. *Refer to Table 14.15*

Chapter Contains	
Total ط	Total س
27 = ط	**93** = س
Chapter Number = **27**	Total Verses = **93**
ط and س	ط and س
Both there in 13 Verses	Not there in 26 Verses
Total Verses = 39 which is a mirror of 93	

Table 14.15

The Curious Case of Letter "waw" (و)

قَالَ سَنَنظُرُ أَصَدَقْتَ أَمْ كُنتَ مِنَ ٱلْكَـٰذِبِينَ ۝

*(Chapter **27 : 27**) - Letters **27**, No 'و'*

- A curious anomaly arises with the letter *'waw'* **و**, the **27**th letter of the Arabic alphabet. Despite its numerical significance, the 27th verse of Chapter 27 is the only verse in the chapter that notably lacks the presence of the 27th letter *'waw'* **و**.

- Adding to the intrigue, the 27th verse consists of precisely 27 letters, echoing the Chapter number and incessantly hinting at the 27th letter *'waw'* و.

The composition of the Quran is indeed a masterpiece, continuing to inspire awe and reverence.

- The letter *'waw'* و continues to unveil its mathematical significance in Chapter 27. The chapter has a total of 93 verses, and verses that begin with the letter *'waw'* و are 33, while the remaining 60 verses commence with other letters. Remarkably, subtracting 33 from 60 yields 27, aligning with both the chapter number and Arabic letter number of *'waw'* و.

Verses that start with Letter و	Other Verses
33 Verses	60 Verses
(60 - 33) = **27** = Chapter Number	

- Further adding to the mystique in Chapter 27, the only verse that contains 9 occurrences of the letter *"waw"* (و) is Verse 3. Remarkably, appending these numbers yields 93 once again, reflecting the total number of verses in the chapter. Multiplying these numbers (9 x 3), we get 27, the Chapter number, reaffirming the marvellous references embedded within its composition.

Digital System and "waw" (و)

The appearance of the Arabic letter *"waw"* (و) in Chapter 27 of the Quran is not just a linguistic feature but a testament to the intricate mathematical structure embedded within the text. It also mirrors the digital system of numbers in mathematics, where the digits 0 to 9 form the basis of all numerical values. The distribution of *"waw"* across the verses of Chapter 27 aligns with this fundamental digital system of 0 to 9. This means that the letter *"waw"* appears between 0 to 9 times in different verses, emphasizing the significance of the numerical composition in the Quran. *Refer to Table 14.16 A*

	Mathematical Precision of 'Waw' (و)										
No. of Times	**0**	**1**	**2**	**3**	**4**	**5**	**6**	**7**	**8**	**9**	
→ In Lines	1	14	13	19	15	14	6	9	1	1	**93**
Total	0	14	26	57	60	70	36	63	8	9	**343**
→		**114131915146911 ÷ 19**									

Table 14.16 A

The letter *"waw"* (و) appears in Chapter 27 with a distinct and impressive mathematical sequence covering all digits from 0 to 9. It appears 0 times in 1 Verse [v.27]. 1 time in 14 Verses, 2 times in 13 verses, 3 times in 19 verses, 4 times in 15 verses, 5 times in 14 verses, 6 times in 6 verses, 7 times in 9 verses, 8 times in 1 verse [v.33] and 9 times in 1 verse [v.3]:

Times	**Verses**	Times	**Verses**	Times	**Verses**
0	1	4	15	7	9
1	14	5	14	8	1
2	13	6	6	9	1
3	19				

Table 14.16 B

This sequence results in a total of 343 occurrences of the letter *"waw,"* which is the cube of 7, expressed as 7^3 or $(7 \times 7 \times 7)$. This sequence becomes even more mind-boggling when the number derived from the verse count 114131915146911 is perfectly divisible by the majestic number 19. *Refer to Table 14.16 A* and *Table 14.16 B*

The Missing Phrase بِسْمِ ٱللَّهِ ٱلرَّحْمَٰنِ ٱلرَّحِيمِ

In the Quran, every chapter begins with the phrase *"Bismillah Ar Rahman Ar Rahim"* (In the name of God, the Most Gracious, the Most

Merciful) as a header or a line, except for Chapter 9 *(At-Tawbah)*. The absence of this sacred phrase in Chapter 9 raises an intriguing question: why is the Quran missing one instance of this phrase, which would seemingly reduce its count to 113, one short of the total number of chapters in the Quran?

The answer to this mystery is resolved 19 chapters later in Chapter 27 *(An-Naml)*, where the phrase *"Bismillah Ar Rahman Ar Rahim"* appears twice. It is present first as the regular header, like in other chapters, but then reappears in verse 27:30. This verse marks the start of a letter written by Prophet *Sulaiman* (Solomon) to the Queen of Saba, where the phrase is used as part of the greeting: *"It is from Sulaiman, and it is [written]:* ***'In the name of God, the Most Gracious, the Most Merciful'.***" The second occurrence of *"Bismillah Ar Rahman Ar Rahim"* in Chapter 27 restores the total count of this phrase in the Quran to 114, perfectly aligning with the number of chapters and maintaining the balance as a multiple of 19.

What makes this even more striking is the mathematical alignment of verse 27:30.

- The sum of the chapter number (27) and verse number (30) equals **57**, which is a multiple of 19.
- Additionally, the number **30** holds special significance as it is the 19th composite number.
- Moreover, Verse 30 has 8 words, the sum of which is **38**, another multiple of 19, reinforcing the Quran's intricate numerical design.

The Word "Qaala" قَال *in Chapter 27*

In Chapter 27, the word *"Qaala"* قَال marks the beginning of Verse 27, just as *"Qaala"* قَال was the first word of Verse 26 of Chapter 26. The significance of the word *"Qaala"* will become clear in the examples that follow.

- The first word of Chapter 27: Verse 27 is *"Qaala"* قَالَ
- Total word count of *"Qaala"* قَالَ in the entire Chapter is 13 times.

Center of the Chapter and the letter ط

½ of Chapter = v. 47 is at	**27:47**
½ of ط (27) = #14 is at	**27:47**

Chapter 27 contains some more interesting patterns. The chapter has a total of 93 verses, with Verse **47** being the center of the chapter. The letter ط appears **27** times in this chapter, and interestingly, its center, the 14th occurrence of ط is at Verse **47**. Thus, the compilation of the chapter is such that the letter ط appears an equal number of times before and after Verse **27:47**, which is also the midpoint of the chapter.

Center of the word "Qaala" قَالَ *and the letter* س

Additionally, the word *"Qaala"* قَالَ occurs 13 times in the chapter, with its center, the 7th occurrence of *"Qaala"* قَالَ at Verse **40**. Similarly, the letter س appears 93 times, and its center, the 47th occurrence of س is also at Verse **40**. So again, the compilation of the chapter is such that the letter س and the word *"Qaala"* appear an equal number of times before and after Verse **27:40**.

½ of Qaala (13) = # 7 is at	**27:40**
½ of س (93) = #47 is at	**27:40**

Appending both the above numbers of the center verses in succession (40 and 47), which are the midpoint of *Muqattaat* letters ط and س, we get **4047**, which is again perfectly divisible by 19 (213 x 19).

Such numerical patterns continue to reinforce the notion that the Quran's composition is beyond human capability, indicating a deliberate and orchestrated design rather than a mere coincidence.

* * *

The Mystery of Chapter 28 - طسم

As we journey further into the Quran, Chapter 28 unfolds another fascinating blend of mathematical precision and divine harmony. This chapter begins with the repeated form of *Muqattaat* طسم, written as a separate verse having a distinct verse number. With 88 verses, Chapter 28 showcases mathematical patterns that affirm the Quran's magnificent arrangement.

Numerical Alignment and Pi

The total number of verses in Chapter 28 is 88. An intriguing correlation emerges with the mathematical constant *Pi* (π). Just as *Pi* is defined as the ratio of the circumference (c) of a circle to its diameter (d), the ratio of the total verses to the chapter number (88 ÷ 28) approximates π, yielding approximately 3.1428. This subtle alignment with *Pi* highlights the chapter's connection to one more fundamental mathematical pattern. Furthermore, appending the chapter number (28) to the total number of verses (88), we get **2888**, a number divisible by 19. *Refer to Table 14.17*

Pi (π)	
Chapter No.	Total Verses
28	**88**
88 ÷ 28 = **π** = 3.1428	
2888 *which is divisible by (÷ 19)*	

Table 14.17

The Distribution of Letters ط س م

Chapter 28 continues to showcase remarkable mathematical patterns through the distribution of the *Muqattaat* letters ط , س and م. *Refer to Table 14.18*

- The letter ط appears exactly **19** times, across 16 verses and the letter س appears 101 times across **57** verses, where 57 is a multiple of 19.
- The letter م is present in all 88 verses, totalling **457** occurrences. Notably, 457 is the 88th prime number, also reflecting the total number of verses in the chapter.
- Additionally, the total *Muqattaat* letters ط س and م until verse 28 of the chapter are 8, 37, and 126, respectively, totalling **171**. This total is also a multiple of 19.

	Chapter 28 Contains		
	Total ط	Total س	Total م
Σ Count	**19** = ط	101 = س	457 = م
In Lines	16	**57**	88
	16 = (2 x 8); 28	57 = (19 x 3)	457 = **88th** Prime No.
Uptill v.28	8	37	126
	Sum of (8 + 37 + 126) = **171** *which is divisible by (÷ 19)*		

Table 14.18

- The last appearance of the letter ط is in verse 82, which is a mirror of the chapter number 28.
- The last occurrence of all three *Muqattaat* letters ط س and م in the same verse is in verse 82, the mirror number of chapter number 28.
- Throughout the chapter, the verse endings are in one of the 4 letters, either ر ل م or ن. The *Hija'i* Alphabet placement of each letter is 10, 23, 24, and 25, respectively. The sum of these numbers equals 82, the mirror number of chapter 28. *Refer to Table 14.19*

	Hijaai Alphabet Count			
Placement	10th	23rd	24th	25th
Letter	ر	ل	م	ن
	(10 + 23 + 24 + 25) = **82**			

Table 14.19

- Out of the 88 verses, 6 end in either م ل ر equally, 2 lines each. The sum of the *Hija'i* Alphabet placement of these 3 letters (10 + 23 + 24) equals **57**, which is divisible by 19. The letter ن marks the end of the remaining 82 lines, which is the mirror of chapter number 28.
- Out of the 6 verses [16, 22, 23, 24, 28,79] with different endings, the first 2 verses, Verse 16 and Verse 22, sum up to 38, which is a multiple of 19. The difference between the mirror numbers of the center 2 verses (42 -32) is 10, and the letter ر which is common to both the verses, is the 10th Arabic Letter. The last 2 verses, Verse 28 and Verse 79, sum up to 107, the 28th prime number, echoing the chapter number. Additionally, the sum of the first and last verses, 16 and 79, equals 95, another multiple of 19. *Refer to Table 14.20*

	Verse Ending Letters					
Verse No.	16	22	23	24	28	79
Ending	م	ل	ر	ر	ل	م
	(16 + 22) = **38**		(42 - 32) = **10**		(28 - 79) = **107**	
	(79 + 16) = **95** *which is divisible by (÷ 19)*					
Total	**Verses Ending with Letter ن = 82 Verses**					

Table 14.20

The Word "Qaala" قَالَ *in Chapter 28*

In a continuation of the pattern observed in previous chapters, the word *"Qaala"* (قَالَ) holds special significance in Chapter 28:

Just as *"Qaala"* (قَالَ) is the first word in Verse 26 of Chapter 26 and the first word in Verse 27 of Chapter 27, it is also the first word in Verse 28 of Chapter 28. This consistent placement suggests that these chapters were intentionally positioned in the Quran exactly where they are. Their arrangement is not random or the result of chance; rather, it reflects a deliberate order within the Quran's composition and compilation.

- The first word of Chapter 28 : Verse 28 is *"Qaala"* قَالَ
- The word *"Qaala"* قَالَ appears a total of **19** times in the chapter.
- The biggest gap between the appearance of the word *"Qaala"* قَالَ in Chapter 28 is found between the 16th and 15th time, which corresponds to Verse 63 and Verse 35, respectively. The difference between these verses (63 – 35) equals 28, which is the chapter number. Interestingly, 1615 is also a perfect multiple of 19.
- The word *"Qaala"* قَالَ appears consecutively in 8 verses from Verse 15 to Verse 23. The sum of the 8 verse numbers equals **171**, which is a multiple of 19 (19 x 9).

15 + 16 + 17 + 18 + **19** + 20 + 21 + 22 + 23 = **171**

- The central verse among these 8 verses is the **19th** verse.
- The maximum number of *Muqattaat* letters (ط س م) in a single verse is 14, which is prevalent in both Verse 15 and Verse 23 in the above sequence. The sum of 15 and 23 equals **38**, a multiple of 19.

The remarkable symmetry, numerical alignments, and consistent patterns across these chapters strengthen our belief in the Quran's divine origin. The meticulous arrangement of verses and letters, the profound significance of *Muqattaat*, and the recurring theme of 19 all point to a higher intelligence guiding the compilation of this sacred text.

In conclusion, Mathematics, as a steadfast guardian of truth, has unveiled the harmony and accord within the Quran, dispelling the shadows of doubt cast by history.

***

The Comparison of Chapters 26, 27, and 28

As we explore deeper and compare Chapters 26, 27, and 28 of the Quran, we uncover a series of intricate mathematical patterns that resonate with the distinctive touch of the Creator. *Refer to Table 14.21*

- All three chapters begin with the Arabic letter ط*(Taa)*
- Their first lines add up to 30 letters, where 30 is the 19th composite number, and their first lines add up to 8 words.
- With 30 Letters and 8 Words, the numbers add up to 38, a multiple of 19.

Chapter	Quran Verse	Letters	Words
26 : 1	طسم	3	1
27 : 1	طسٓ ۚ تِلْكَ آيَاتُ ٱلْقُرْآنِ وَكِتَابٍ مُّبِينٍ	24	6
28 : 1	طسم	3	1
	Σ Total =	**30**	**8**

Table 14.21

- All three chapters end with the letter ن *"Noon"*, and their final wordsينقلبون , تعملون , ترجعون have a total of 19 letters. *Refer to Table 14.22*

	Chapter 26	Chapter 27	Chapter 28
End Word	يَنقَلِبُونَ	تَعْمَلُونَ	تُرْجَعُونَ
Count	**7** Letters	**6** Letters	**6** Letters

(7 + 6 + 6) =**19** Letters

Table 14.22

- Chapters 26 and 27 both contain an equal **93** instances of the letter س *"Seen"*, despite varying lengths, 227 verses of Chapter 26 and 93 of Chapter 27. *Refer to Table 14.23*

	Chapter 26	Chapter 27
Letter	س	س
Total	93	93

Equal

Table 14.23

- Chapters 27 and 28 combined have an equal number of the letters ط*(Taa)* and س*(Seen)* - **120** occurrences each. *Refer to Table 14.23-B*
- Chapter 27 has 93 "س" and 27 "ط", which adds to **120**
- Chapter 28 has 101 "س" and 19 "ط", which also adds to **120**

	Chapter 27	Chapter 28
Letter	ط + س	ط + س
Total	93 + 27 = **120**	101 + 19 = **120**

Equal

Table 14.23-B

- Chapter 27, which begins with ط and س *(Taa Seen)*, has **13** verses that contain both letters of *Muqattaat*
- Chapter 28, which begins with طسم*(Taa Seen Meem)*, also has **13** verses containing all three letters. *Refer to Table 14.24*

Verses in Chapter **27** having ط س

Count	*1*	*2*	*3*	*4*	*5*	*6*	*7*	*8*	*9*	*10*	*11*	*12*	**13**
Verse No.	1	7	16	21	22	24	40	48	56	58	59	62	68

Verses in Chapter **28** having ط س م

Count	*1*	*2*	*3*	*4*	*5*	*6*	*7*	*8*	*9*	*10*	*11*	*12*	**13**
Verse No.	1	4	10	15	19	23	29	30	35	38	45	58	82

Table 14.24

The Word "Allah"

• Another astonishing fact is that in Chapters 26, 27, and 28, the word *"Allah"* appears for the first time in Verses 89, 8, and 13, respectively. All 3 are numbers in the Fibonacci series. Appending these numbers, we get **89813**, which is perfectly divisible by 19.

• The last appearance of the word *"Allah"* in the 3 chapters is in Verses 227, 88 and 88, respectively. Expressing these numbers using math operators yields (227 x 88 + 88), which equals **20064**, a multiple of 19.

• The total count of the word *"Allah"* in Chapters 26, 27, and 28 is 13, 22, and 26 times, respectively. Appending these numbers results in 132226, and its mirror number, **622231**, is a perfect multiple of 19.

• In Chapters 26, 27, and 28, the only verse that begins with the word *"Allah"* is found in Chapter 27, verse 26. The verse is located in Juz' 19, concludes with a' Sajda, comprises 27 letters and 8 words. The difference between the number of letters and the words (27 - 8) is **19**.

Placement of "Qaala"

The word *" Qaala"* قَالَ appears as the first word in Verses 26:26, 27:27, 28:28, and 19:19. The word *"Qaala"* in these chapters serves as a key indicator of the chapter's position in the Quran.

▪ *" Qaala"* قَالَ is the **1**st word of Chapter **26**, Verse **26**
▪ *" Qaala"* قَالَ is the **1**st word of Chapter **27**, Verse **27**
▪ *" Qaala"* قَالَ is the **1**st word of Chapter **28**, Verse **28**
▪ *" Qaala"* قَالَ is the **1**st word of Chapter **19**, Verse **19**

This further exemplifies the deliberate placement of the word *" Qaala"* قَالَ within the Quran. The fact that both the verse number and chapter number are the same emphasizes that the position of these chapters, 26,

27, 28, and 19, is not random but intentionally arranged. It is another powerful hint towards the divine design of the Quran's compilation.

In our search for truth, the intricate mathematical patterns embedded within the Quran strongly suggest that its composition, compilation, and completeness are intact. The Quran we hold today appears to be the same as the one left behind by Prophet Muhammed (S), same as the one aligning with the "book of God" mentioned in *Hadith al-Thaqalayn*, where Prophet Muhammed (S), in his final sermon, stated: *"Indeed, I am leaving two things among you, to which if you hold yourself, you will never astray:* ***the book of God*** *and my ahl al-bayt (household), my 'itra (family)."*

All the mathematical evidence and profound numerical patterns emphasise the Quran's authenticity and preservation, reinforcing our belief in its divine origin and unaltered transmission through the ages.

* * *

The Mystery of Chapter 36 - "Ya-seen" يسٓ

The Heart of the Quran

Chapter 36, *"Ya-seen"* (يسٓ) is one of the most prominent chapters in the Quran, widely known as the heart of the Quran. This distinction arises not only from its spiritual significance but also because it is associated with Prophet Muhammed (S), as *"Ya-seen" is* one of his names.

The Beginning Letters

This chapter begins with the well-known two-letter *Muqattaat "Ya-seen"* (**يس**), written as a separate verse and carrying a verse number. This unique beginning also forms the name of the chapter *"Ya-seen"* (**يس**) and its first verse is represented as 36:1. When these numbers are combined, they form 361, which is 19 x 19, the perfect square of 19.

The Numerical Elegance

Ya-seen (يس) is the 36th Chapter of the Quran, and the number 36 equals 6 x 6, or the square of 6. *Ya-seen* has a total of 83 verses. Interestingly, the mirror number of 83 is 38, divisible by 19. Even more fascinating is that *Ya-seen,* which is Chapter 36, has a total of 83 verses, whereas Chapter 83 contains 36 verses. This creates a mirrored relationship between the chapter numbers and their verses.

Mirror Chapters	
Chapter **36**	Chapter 83
Verses 83	Verses **36**

The Connection to Prophet Muhammed (S)

The chapter and the letters *"Ya-seen"* (يس) are significant for their association with Prophet *Muhammed* (S), as *Ya-seen* is one of his names.

This chapter not only honours him but also subtly refers to another chapter named after him: Chapter 47, titled *"Muhammed"*, which contains 38 verses, a multiple of 19.

Chapter 36 contains a total of 235 instances of the *Muqattaat* letter ي *(Ya)*, which is perfectly divisible by 47. There are 47 instances of the letter س *(Seen)* in the chapter. The combined total of both letters is 282, which is 47 multiplied by 6. This highlights the importance of both the numbers 47 and 6 within the chapter. *Refer to Table 14.25*

	Chapter Contains	
	Total ي	Total س
Count	235 (**47** x 5)	**47**
Σ	Total (235 + 47) = **282** = (**47** x **6**)	

Table 14.25

- The difference between the total number of verses (83) and the chapter number (36) is also **47** (83-36).
- Verse 6 is unique as it is the only verse that contains neither the letter *"Ya"(*ي) nor *"Seen"(*س). This is the only verse in the entire chapter that has no letters of the opening *Muqattaat. Refer to Table 14.26*
- Verse 47 is unique as it has exactly 6 instances of "ي" and no "س".

	Verse Contains		
	Verse No.	ي	س
Unique	6	0	0
	47	6	0

Table 14.26

- The first 6 verses contain (1 + 2 + 3 + 3 + 3 + 7) exactly 19 words, aligning with the majestic number 19. *Refer to Table 14.27*

Chapter - 36 Ya-Seen		
Line	بِسْمِ ٱللَّهِ ٱلرَّحْمَـٰنِ ٱلرَّحِيمِ	Words
1	يسٓ ۞	1
2	وَٱلْقُرْءَانِ ٱلْحَكِيمِ ۞	2
3	إِنَّكَ لَمِنَ ٱلْمُرْسَلِينَ ۞	3
4	عَلَىٰ صِرَٰطٍ مُّسْتَقِيمٍ ۞	3
5	تَنزِيلَ ٱلْعَزِيزِ ٱلرَّحِيمِ ۞	3
6	۞ لِتُنذِرَ قَوْمًا مَّآ أُنذِرَ ءَابَآؤُهُمْ فَهُمْ غَـٰفِلُونَ ۞	7
	Σ TOTAL WORDS UP TILL 6 LINES =	**19**

Table 14.27

- There are 5 verses (38, 47, 50, 65, and 66) where both *"Ya"*(ي) and *"Seen"*(س) add up to 6 Letters in the verse. Adding these verse numbers totals **266**, which is divisible by 19. *Refer to Table 14.28*

Verse Contains			
Verse No.	س	ي	Total
38	2	4	6
47	0	6	6
50	1	5	6
65	1	5	6
66	2	4	6

(19 x 14) **266** = TOTAL OF VERSE NUMBERS

Table 14.28

- There are 4 verses (20, 30, 40, and 81) where both *"Ya"*(ي) and *"Seen"*(س) add up to 8 Letters in the verse. Adding these verse numbers totals **171**, which is divisible by 19. *Refer to Table 14.29*

Verse Contains			
Verse No.	س	ي	Total
20	2	6	8
30	3	5	8
40	3	5	8
81	2	6	8

(19 x 9) **171** = TOTAL OF VERSE NUMBERS

Table 14.29

Divine Pairs in 36:36

Verse 36:36 of the Quran speaks about pairs, and intriguingly, its structure reflects this theme of duality.

س ى س ى

سُبْحَـٰنَ ٱلَّذِى خَلَقَ ٱلْأَزْوَٰجَ كُلَّهَا مِمَّا تُنۢبِتُ ٱلْأَرْضُ وَمِنْ أَنفُسِهِمْ وَمِمَّا لَا يَعْلَمُونَ ۝

36:36 *Glory be to the One Who created all things* ***in pairs...***

- In verse number 36:36, the numbers themselves form a visible pair.

- The verse contains 55 letters, illustrating another pair of numbers.
- Within the verse, there are 2 occurrences of the letters "ي" *(Ya)* and 2 occurrences of "س" *(Seen)*, which are the *Muqattaat* (disjointed letters) that appear in pairs at the beginning of Chapter 36.
- The difference between the verse number (36) and the number of letters (55) is exactly 19.

This elegant mathematical symmetry highlights the profound depth and precision of the Quran's composition.

***

The Mystery of The Twin Chapters 50 and 42

Chapters 50 and 42 of the Quran are related as they both have the *Muqattaat* letter "*Qaf*" (ق). Comparing the mathematical patterns within these chapters reveals a remarkable mathematical harmony, showcasing the Quran's intricate composition.

Chapter 50 - "Qaf" (ق)

Chapter 50 is named "*Qaf*" (ق) and begins with the unique *Muqattaat* "*Qaf*" (ق), seamlessly attached to the first verse, unlike many other chapters where the Muqattaat letters are written as separate verses.

Chapter 42: Ash-Shura

Similarly, Chapter 42 (Ash-Shura) opens with a unique *Muqattaat* sequence عسق, which is listed as the 2nd verse, with the letter "*Qaf*" (ق) appearing prominently at the end of the *Muqattaat.*

The Mathematical Symmetry

When examining the occurrences of the letter "*Qaf*" (ق), in both chapters, a remarkable symmetry emerges:

Equal "Qaf" ق In Chapters		
	Chapter 42	Chapter 50
(÷ 19)	**57 ق**	**57 ق**

Total ق in both the Chapters = 114 (19 x 6)

- Both chapters (42 and 50) contain the letter "*Qaf*" (ق) equally - **57** times. This number is not arbitrary; 57 is a multiple of 19, a recurring number in the Quran's mathematical patterns.
- The total occurrences of ق in Chapters 42 and 50 combined is (57 + 57), which is **114**, which equals the total number of chapters in the Quran.

Equal Distribution.

The plot thickens as the equal distribution of Chapter Numbers and Verses continues. *Refer to Table 14.30,*

Equal Distribution		
	Chapter 42	Chapter 50
	Total Verses = 53	Total Verses = 45
(÷ 19)	(42 + 53) = **95**	(50 + 45) = **95**

(95 + 95) = 190

Table 14.30

- Chapter 42 has 53 verses. Adding the chapter number to the verse count yields **95** (42 + 53), a multiple of 19.

- Chapter 50 has 45 verses. Similarly, adding the chapter number to the verse count also results in **95** (50 + 45), a multiple of 19.
- The total of both chapter numbers and their respective verses is **190** (95 + 95), reinforcing the consistent presence of 19.

Differences in Numbers:

We continue to compare Chapters 50 and 42, considering them to be lookalikes.

Equal Differences	
Chapter 42	Total Verses = 53
Chapter 50	Total Verses = 45
(50 - 42) = **8**	(53 – 45) = **8**

8th Prime Number = **19**

Table 14.31

- The difference between the chapter numbers (50 - 42) is 8 and the difference between their verse counts (53 - 45) is also 8. Notably, the 8th Prime Number is 19. *Refer to Table 14.31*

Equal in Reverse / Mirror

A CHAPTER

Chapter 42	Chapter 50
Reverse : 24	Reverse : 05

(24 - 05) = **19**

B VERSES

Verses 53	Verses 45
Reverse : 35	Reverse : 54

(54 - 35) = **19**

Table 14.32

- When the chapter numbers are reversed (42 to 24 and 50 to 05), their difference (24 - 05) becomes **19**. Similarly, reversing or mirroring the verse numbers (53 to 35 and 45 to 54) also yields a difference (54 - 35) of **19**. *Refer to Table 14.32*

* * *

Is Number 19 a Coincidence in Muqattaat?

Beneath the enigma of Muqattaat, there lies a trail of patterns too precise to dismiss. There are 2 ways of counting the letters of the Muqattaat: counting their presence, either within the 78-letter span of all Muqattaat (*Refer to Table 14.1)* or counting their numbers within the 143 letters of the Key Chapter 1, *Surah al-Hamd.* Since all 14 letters of the Muqattaat are a part of *Surah al-Hamd,* we can also count the occurrence of the Muqattaat letters within Chapter 1. *Refer to Table 14.33*

أ 26	ح 5	ر 8	س 3	ص 2	ط 2	ع 6
ق 1	ك 3	ل 22	م 15	ن 11	ه 5	ي 14

Table 14.33: Count of Letters of Muqattaat **in *Surah al-Hamd***

Notably, the Muqattaat letters أ ل ر (A.L.R.), appearing in 5 chapters, occur 13, 13, and 6 times, respectively, in the total Muqattaat. When these occurrences are combined, it forms 13136, whose mirror number is **61313**, which neatly divides into 19 without a remainder.

Now shifting the lens to the 13 chapters, where Muqattaats begin with أ ل (A.L.), the occurrences of these 2 letters in *Surah al-Hamd* stand at 26 for أ (A) and 22 for ل (L), forming the number **2622**, which is again divisible by 19.

The counts of the letters of Muqattaat أ ل م (A.L.M) in *Surah al-Hamd* are 26, 22, and 15. Expressing this with operators (26 - 22 + 15) equals 19. *Refer to Table 14.33*

The chapter numbers [40, 41, 43, 44, 45, 46] that are headed by ح م (HM), when clubbed together in reverse order, form 464544434140, which is divisible by 19.

The Mystery of the Hidden Code in Chapter 19

- Even the Muqattaat in Chapter 19 ك ه ي ع ص (k. h. Y. a. s) echo this pattern. Their counts in *Surah al-Hamd* are 3, 5, 14, 6, and 2, respectively, which can be combined as **351462**. This number is just another whisper of 19, another number perfectly divisible by 19, like a key fitting a lock.
- When we add all the counts together **(3 + 5 + 14 + 6 + 2)**, the total is **30**, which is the 19th composite number.
- In Chapter 19, there is **1** line [verse **88]** that does not contain any of the five letters of the Muqattaat, whereas **9** lines in the chapter consist of all five letters of the Muqattaat. These verses are:

  [1, 14, 36, 38, 42, 43, 54, 55, 76]

  This combination of 1 and 9 lines, without and with the letters of the Muqattaat, resonates with the number 19. Furthermore, the first digits of the line numbers containing all five letters of the Muqattaat form a number, **113344557**, which is a multiple of 19.

The Mystery of the Hidden Code in ص *(Saad)*

Among the mysterious Muqattaat letters that open several chapters of the Quran, the letter ص *(Saad)* stands as a peculiar and powerful symbol, quietly carrying within it a mathematical fingerprint. This letter appears as a Muqattaat at the beginning of only three chapters: Chapter 7 *(Al-A'raf)*, Chapter 19 *(Maryam)*, and Chapter 38 *(Saad)*.

Yet when we turn to numbers, a different kind of clarity begins to surface.

- In Chapters 7, 19, and 38, the letter ص *(Saad)* appears 97, 26, and 29 times, respectively. These are not random figures; when added, they equal a total of **152**, a number divisible by 19. But the intrigue doesn't end there. The actual sequence of these occurrences (97, 26, and 29) stringed together forms the number **972629**. This number also turns out to be perfectly divisible by 19. *Refer to Table 14.34*

Muqattaat ص						
	C		V	C+V	C-V	ص
#1	7	:	206	213	199	97
#2	19	:	98	117	79	26
#3	38	:	88	126	-50	29
TOTAL				456	228	152

VISIBLE SEQUENCE

C	C	V	V	V
	7	2	0	6
1	9	9	8	
3	8	8	8	

↑ 318978928806 ÷ 19

Table 14.34

- The three Chapters (7, 19, 38) that contain the Muqattaat ص *(Saad)* have 206, 98, and 88 verses, respectively. The sum of all the chapter and verse numbers (7 + 19 + 38 + 206 + 98 + 88) equals **456**, and the sum of the differences of the chapter and verse numbers equals **228**; both 456 and 228 are perfect multiples of 19.
- The numbers written as a continuous string, as seen column-wise, form **318978928806**, which is divisible by 19.

The recurrence of the number 19 through different paths, in various examples, along with the symmetrical letters and distribution of words, are not mere coincidences but significant indicators of the Quran's authenticity and preservation.

15

OVER IT ARE NINETEEN

For centuries, history has carried the weight of doubt about the completeness of the Quran. Scholars, critics, and skeptics alike have argued that the Quran we have today is incomplete or altered. Claims of lost verses, missing chapters, or unauthorized changes have echoed through time, bolstered by scattered reports and historical controversies. But now, as the dust of speculation begins to settle, a different kind of witness steps forward: Mathematics.

Among the most intriguing verses in the Quran is the mysterious statement from Chapter 74, verse 30: **"Over it are Nineteen"**. The mathematical correlation of this statement to verse 30 is that the number 30 is incidentally the 19th composite number.

For a long time, this verse stood like a silent monument, unexplained, cryptic, and untouched by traditional exegesis. History chose not to explain it. The narrators fell silent. But where words falter, numbers begin to speak.

What does "Over it are Nineteen" truly mean? No scholar, no historian, no classical commentary offers a definitive explanation. Perhaps it was meant to be that way. Perhaps the meaning was left hidden for a different kind of exploration, a mathematical one.

We already know that the number 19 is not just another numeral in the Quran. It serves as a sign and a seal, as well as a **structural framework**. But can it also be the **connection**, the **link**, between specific words, chapters, and verses in the Quran? Can 19 help reveal how certain divine phrases are sewn into the very architecture of the book of God? Let us explore some fascinating examples of how words connect to the number 19. Let us explore diversified examples to eliminate the possibility of cherry-picking and provide clear evidence that the observed occurrences far exceed random chances.

Case #1 - *Iqra - "Read"* **(اقرَأ)**

The first word revealed to Prophet Muhammed (S) was *"Iqra"* - "Read." This was the launch of a revelation, a divine invitation to seek knowledge, reflect, and uncover the truth. But beyond the linguistic beauty of this word lies something more, an astonishing mathematical echo that pulses quietly through its appearances in the Quran. The word *"Iqra"* (اقرَأ) is the beginning of the first **19** words of the first 5 lines that were revealed to Prophet Muhammed (S). It appears only three times in the Quran: in Surah **17:14**, Surah **96:1**, and Surah **96:3**. *Refer to Table 15.1*

Iqra					
	C		V	C+V	C-V
#1	17	:	14	31	3
#2	96	:	1	97	95
#3	96	:	3	99	93
Σ	209		18	227	191
Σu	113 - 18				95

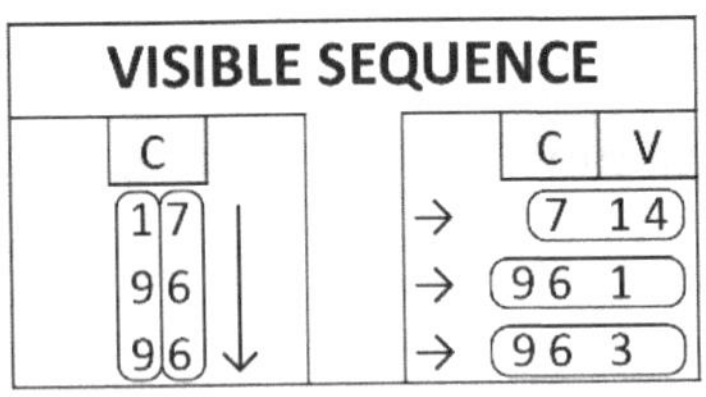

↓ 199766 ÷ 19

→ 714961963 ÷ 19

[(1714 x 961) + 963] = 1648117 ÷ **19**

Table 15.1

At first glance, these may appear like ordinary references. But for those following the thread of mathematics, each placement feels like a precisely placed pin in a divine blueprint.

- The difference between the chapter and verse numbers in the second occurrence 96:1 is (96 – 1) **95**, which is divisible by 19.
- The sum of the chapter numbers of all three occurrences (17 + 96 + 96) is **209**, another multiple of 19.
- If we exclude the repeated chapter, the sum of the unique chapter numbers (17 + 96) becomes 113, while the sum of the verse numbers (14 + 1 + 3) is 18. The difference between these two values (113 –18) is **95**, again divisible by 19.
- Applying math operators to the occurrences gives: ((1714 × 961) + 963), which equals **1648117**, a number divisible by19.
- When we queue the numbers and exclude the first digit (1), there is a hidden number, we get **714961963**. This, too, aligns perfectly with the mathematical fingerprint of 19.
- And when we observe the chapter numbers column-wise, written as a continuous string, we get **199766**, again divisible by 19.

* * *

Case #2 - *Kun Fa Yakun - "Be, and it is"* (كُن فَيَكونُ)

Among the most powerful phrases in the Quran is *Kun Fa Yakun*, "Be, and it is." A simple yet profound declaration of divine authority. It echoes not just as a statement of creation but as a glimpse into the effortless command of the Creator. Interestingly, while its meaning is universal and absolute, its appearances in the Quran seem to follow a very particular mathematical pattern. *Refer to Table 15.2*

This phrase occurs **eight times** across the Quran: in **2:117**, **3:47**, **3:59**, **6:73**, **16:40**, **19:35**, **36:82**, and **40:68**. When we sum all the **chapter**

numbers, the result is **125**, and the sum of all the **verse numbers** is **521**. The numbers 125 and 521 are mirror numbers of one another. The combined total (125 + 521) is **646**, a number that divides cleanly by **19**.

Kun fa Yakun					
	C		V	C+V	V-C
#1	2	:	117	119	115
#2	3	:	47	50	44
#3	3	:	59	62	56
#4	6	:	73	79	67
#5	16	:	40	56	24
#6	19	:	35	54	16
#7	36	:	82	118	46
#8	40	:	68	108	28
Σ	**125**	**<>**	**521**	**646**	396
Σu	**122**	**-**	**521**	643	**399**

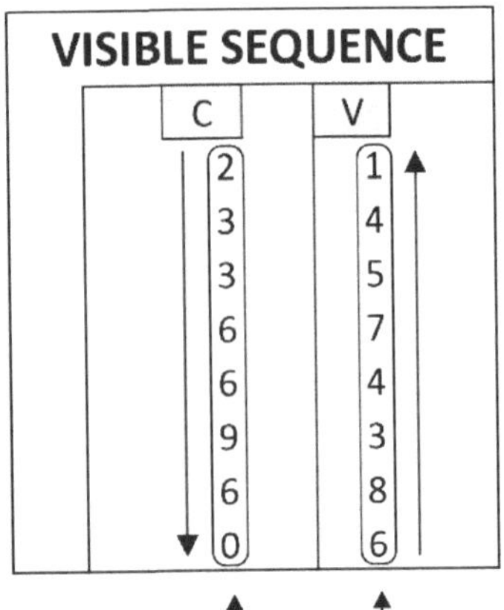

↓ 23366960 ÷ **19**

↑ 68347541 ÷ **19**

Table 15.2

Looking at the first and last occurrence, from Chapter 2 to Chapter 40, the difference between these chapter numbers (40 – 2) is **38**, which again is divisible by 19, the divine watermark.

When we exclude the repeated chapters and consider only the sum of unique chapter numbers, the total amounts to 122. The difference between the sum of unique chapter numbers and the sum of all verse numbers (521 – 122) is **399**. Interestingly, 399 is also divisible by 19.

And surprisingly, when all the chapter numbers and verse numbers are aligned in columns, in the second column of the chapter numbers, we find the number **23366960.** Once again, we find a number that follows the established pattern and is perfectly divisible by 19.

In the second column of the verse numbers, we see another wonder, the number **68347541** in reverse, and once again, we have stumbled upon a number perfectly divisible by 19.

* * *

Case #3 - Waraq al-Jannah - "*Leaves of Paradise*" **(وَرَقِ الجَنَّةِ)**

The Quran narrates an important story when Prophet Adam and Eve, deceived by Satan, covered themselves with the leaves of Paradise, referred to as *"Waraq al-Jannah."* This phrase appears only twice in the entire Quran, in Chapter 7, Verse 22 **(7:22)** and Chapter 20, Verse 121 **(20:121)**. At first glance, these references appear simple, but a deeper analysis reveals some extraordinary mathematics. *Refer to Table 15.3*

Leaves of Paradise				
	C		V	Append
#1	7	:	22	722
#2	20	:	121	20121
TOTAL	**27**		**143**	
	→ 722 + 20121 = 20843			
	→ 20121 - 722 = 19399			

VISIBLE SEQUENCE
→ 722 ÷ 19
→ 20121 ÷ 19
<> **27341** ÷ 19 (Mirror)
↑ 12122 ÷ 19 (Verses)

Table 15.3

- As appended numbers, both **722** and **20121** are perfectly divisible by 19, the recurring numerical seal stamped throughout the Quran.
- But the marvel doesn't end there. Combining just the verse numbers themselves, 121 and 22, results in **12122**, which is divisible by 19.
- Furthermore, the sum of these two numbers (722 + 20121) results in **20843**, and their difference (20121 -722) results in **19399**, both of which are naturally divisible by 19.

What seems to be a simple, symbolic reference to the leaves of paradise carries a subtle mathematical link with strong evidence suggesting that the occurrences are not random.

* * *

Case #4 - Al-Yakeen - "*Certainity*" **(اليَقين)**

The word **"Al-Yakeen"**—meaning *certainty*, appears six times in the Quran, at the **end of the verse**, signifying a strong concluding message. These verses occur in **15:99, 56:95, 69:51, 74:47, 102:5, and 102:7**. What stands out beyond the message is the remarkable numerical harmony these occurrences share with the number 19. *Refer to Table 15.4*

Al Yakeen					
	C		V	C+V	V-C
#1	15	:	99	114	84
#2	56	:	95	151	39
#3	69	:	51	120	18
#4	74	<>	47	121	27
#5	102	:	5	107	97
#6	102	:	7	109	95
Σ	418	+	304	722	
Σ	418	-	304	114	

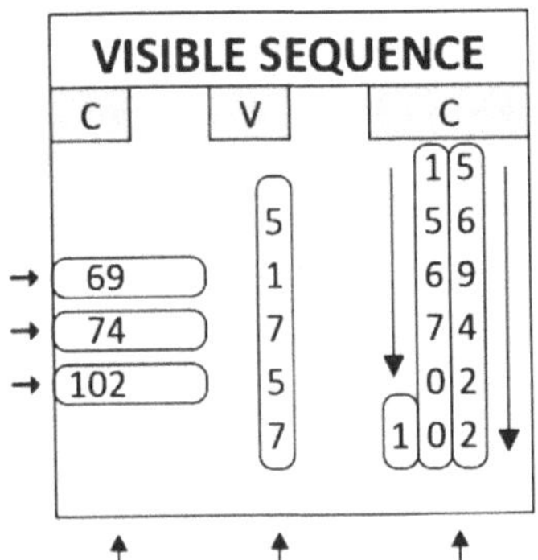

→ 6974102 ÷ 19

→ 75715 ÷ 19

→ 1156700569422 ÷ 19

(418 - 304) = 114 ÷ 19

(1599 + 5695 – 6951 – 7447 + 1025 – 1027) = 7106÷ 19

Table 15.4

- The sum of all chapter numbers—15, 56, 69, 74, 102, and 102 is **418**, a multiple of 19.
- The sum of the verse numbers—99, 95, 51, 47, 5, and 7 equals **304**, also divisible by 19. Their combined total (418 + 304) is **722**, and even their difference (418 – 304) is **114**, a multiple of 19.

- The mathematical symmetry continues when the last three-chapter numbers are treated as a sequence: 69, 74, and 102, and joined as **6974102**, forming again a number divisible by 19.
- Further, there is a hidden structural alignment if we compile all the digits of the chapter numbers in columns, except the first digit (1), that is, excluding '1' from columns of the chapter numbers, we arrive at a large number,**1156700569422,** which is also divisible by 19. This reveals an encoded depth that cannot be easily dismissed as a coincidence.
- When mathematical operations are performed on the combined numbers of the six verse references of *"Al-Yakeen",* specifically,

  (1599 + 5695 – 6951 – 7447 + 1025 – 1027)

  The result of this is **7106**, which again succumbs to the reign of 19.
- Even isolated pairings reveal the same signature: the sum of the chapter and verse from the first occurrence, (15 + 99), yields **114**, the total number of Quranic chapters, and a number divisible by 19.
- The difference between the chapter and verse in the final occurrence (102 – 7) gives **95**, again divisible by 19.

All this suggests that *certainty*, or *al-yakeen*, in the Quran is not just a concept conveyed in words, but mathematically embedded in its very structure—repeated, calculated, and ultimately pointing back to a pattern encoded with precision.

* * *

Case #5 - Shaair - *"Poet"* **(شاعِر)**

The Quran mentions the word **"Shaair"**, meaning *poet*, only four times, and each time it does, it seems to quietly push a deeper design beneath the surface. These occurrences are found in **21:5, 37:36, 52:30**, and **69:41**. *Refer to Table 15.5*

	Shaair				
	C		V	C+V	V-C
#1	21	:	5	26	16
#2	37	:	36	73	1
#3	52	:	30	82	22
#4	69	:	41	110	28

VISIBLE SEQUENCE

C		C	V
2	1	1	5
3	7	37	36
5	2	52	30
6	9	69	41

- → 2356 ÷ 19
- → 1729 ÷ 19
- → 13752695363041 ÷ 19

(215 + 3736 - 5230 + 6941) = 5662 ÷ **19**

Table 15.5

- Start with the chapter numbers 21, 37, 52, and 69. When positioned in columns, they form two distinct four-digit numbers: **2356** and **1729**. Both are divisible by 19, and 1729 is particularly notable as it is a familiar number to us. It holds unique importance both mathematically and contextually. It is the product of 19 × 91, and also the structure of Chapter 1 of the Quran.
- If the first digit (2) is excluded, another hidden figure derived from all the chapter and verse numbers is the number **13752695363041**, which is also divisible by 19.
- When mathematical operations are performed on the numerical references of all four appearances of *"Shaair"*, it can be expressed as: (215 + 3736 - 5230 + 6941), which results in **5662**, divisible by 19. The sum of its digits (5 + 6 + 6 + 2) also adds to 19.

So, within the Quran, the word *Shaair* is enveloped within its unique poetic structure, one written not in rhyme and rhythm, but rather in **the language of numbers**, where the number 19 is subtly concealed.

* * *

Case #6 - Zaalikal Fawzul Azeem - *" that is the supreme success"* (ذَٰلِكَ الفَوزُ العَظِيم)

Zaalikal Fawzul Azeem	C		V	C+V	V-C
#1	**4**	:	13	17	**9**
#2	5	:	119	124	**114**
#3	**9**	:	89	98	80
#4	**9**	:	**100**	109	91
#5	61	:	12	73	**49**
#6	**64**	:	**9**	73	55
	152	**+**	**342**	**494**	**398**
	152	**-**	**342**	**190**	

VISIBLE SEQUENCE

C	C V	C
4	4 1	
5	5 1	
9	9 8	9
9	9 1	9
1	1 1	1
4	4 9	4

→ 459914 ÷ **19**
→ 415198911149 ÷ **19**
↑ 4199 ÷ **19**
→ 413649 ÷ **19**

Table 15.6

In the sacred verses of the Quran, the phrase **"Zaalikal Fawzul Azeem"**— *"That is the supreme success"*, echoes six times like a rhythmic reminder of the ultimate goal. At first glance, its placements at verses **4:13, 5:119, 9:89, 9:100, 61:12, and 64:9** appear to be a poetic arrangement. But beneath the surface lies an astonishing mathematical design, waiting to be discovered. *Refer to Table 15.6*

- The sum of the chapter numbers (4 + 5 + 9 + 9 + 61 + 64) equals **152**, a number directly related to the prime structure of 19.
- Next, the verses themselves (13 + 119 + 89 + 100 + 12 + 9) sum up to **342**, again a perfect multiple of 19. When both the sums are added (152 + 342 = 494) or subtracted (342 - 152 = 190), the result remains divisible by 19. Coincidence? Or design?
- Stack the chapter numbers vertically; the second column combines into **459914**, which is once again divisible by 19.

- Line up the chapter and verse numbers side by side into columns; the two center columns horizontally combine to form a number, **415198911149**, that follows the rhythm of divisibility by 19.
- Finally, the first and last placements, 4:13 and 64:9, join hands to create **413649**, a big piece in this divine puzzle, again perfectly divisible by 19.

Even with this brief understanding, one can only pause and reflect on the words of the Quran : **"Which of your Lord's signs will you deny?"**

* * *

Case #7- *In the Name of God, the Gracious, the Merciful*
(بِسْمِ ٱللَّهِ ٱلرَّحْمَٰنِ ٱلرَّحِيمِ)

If the fingerprint of the number 19 truly weaves through the Quran, then it must surely extend to the most fundamental phrase in the Quran and in Islam: "**Bismillah Ar-Rahman Ar-Rahim**", *In the name of God, the Most Gracious, the Most Merciful.* Refer to Table 15.7

While this phrase is a header or starter to every chapter except Chapter 9, it formally appears only twice as part of the Quranic text, once as **verse 1:1**, and the second, unexpectedly, in **27:30**, where Prophet Solomon writes a letter beginning with "بِسْمِ ٱللَّهِ ٱلرَّحْمَٰنِ ٱلرَّحِيمِ". This dual appearance seems modest, but when we apply the same lens of mathematical reasoning as before, a hidden pattern begins to emerge.

بِسْمِ ٱللَّهِ ٱلرَّحْمَٰنِ ٱلرَّحِيمِ						
	C		V	C+V	C-V	
#1	1	:	1	2	0	
#2	27	:	30	**57**	3	
	28		**31**			→

VISIBLE - SEQUENCE	
	→ 271130 ÷ 19
	→ 12730 ÷ 19
→	→ **2831** ÷ 19

(2730 - 11) = 2719, where (2 + 7 + 1 + 9) = **19**

Table 15.7

- Verse 27:30 contains the number **30**, which is the 19th composite number, quietly anchored to the verse number.
- Add the chapter and verse numbers together (27 + 30); the result is **57**, which is another perfect multiple of 19.
- Diving deeper, we observe that the sum of the chapter numbers: 1 and 27 gives us 28, while the verse numbers, 1 and 30, yield 31. When we combine these totals, we get **2831**, a number that seamlessly fits into an arithmetic structure of 19, skilfully hidden in plain sight.
- Perhaps the most poetic number of all is **271130**, a sequence that combines 1, 1, 27, and 30, representing the chapter and verse numbers of both occurrences. It contains all the referred digits and is also divisible by 19, like a signature sealed within numbers.
- Finally, the difference of the combined numbers (2730 – 11) equals **2719**, where the sum of its digits (2 + 7 + 1 + 9) equals 19.

* * *

Case #8 - Al Balaghul Mubeen- *"The Clear Message"* **(البَلٰغُ المُبِين)**

The phrase **"Al Balaghul Mubeen",** meaning "The Clear Message", appears precisely **seven times** across the Quran. These are found at **5:92**, **16:35**, **16:82**, **24:54**, **29:18**, **36:17**, **64:12**. These phrases are not scattered randomly but are well arranged. *Refer to Table 15.8*

- The sum of the chapter numbers is **190**, a direct multiple of 19.
- The mathematical beauty is highlighted in the units column of the chapter numbers, where, 5, 6, 6, 4, 9, 6, and 4, form the number **5664964**, which, incredibly, is divisible by 19.
- Similarly, the digits extracted from the units column of the verse numbers, that is, 2, 5, 2, 4, 8, 7, and 2, forms **2524872**, another multiple of 19.

Balaghul Mubeen					
	C		V	C+V	C-V
#1	5	:	92	97	87
#2	16	:	35	51	19
#3	16	:	82	98	66
#4	24	:	54	78	30
#5	29	:	18	47	11
#6	36	:	17	53	19
#7	64	:	12	76	52
	190				

VISIBLE SEQUENCE			
C	V	C	V
5	2		
6	5		3
6	2	1	8
4	4	2	5
9	8	2	1
6	7	3	1
4	2	6	1

↓	5664964 ÷ 19
↓	2524872 ÷ 19
↓	12236 ÷ 19
↓	385111 ÷ 19
→	5921635 ÷ 19

Table 15.8

- If the first digit (1) in the tens column of the Chapter numbers is excluded, the pattern continues, and we are left with the numbers 1, 2, 2, 3, and 6, forming **12236**, again divisible by 19.
- Similarly, if the first digit (9) in the tens column of the Verse numbers is excluded, it gives us 3, 8, 5, 1, 1, and 1, forming the number **385111**, which also concedes to being divisible by 19.
- If the chapter and verse numbers of the first two occurrences are combined, they form **5921635**, a number divisible by 19.
- The pattern does not stop here. Subtracting the first occurrence from the sum of all other occurrences of the phrase *"Al Balaghul Mubeen"*, we get: (1635 + 1682 + 2454 + 2918 + 3617 + 6412 - 592), which equals **18126**, yet again, perfectly divisible by 19.

These multiple examples are not mere coincidences; they are mathematical footprints of a design far beyond human creation. The phrase "the clear message" applies not only to the message and meaning of the Quran, but also to the mathematics surrounding the number 19.

* * *

Case #9 - Fattaqullaha wa Aṭi'ūn - *"So fear God and obey me."*

(فَاتَّقُوا اللَّهَ وَأَطِيعُونِ)

For the skeptic mind still clinging to coincidence or resisting the idea of a mathematical signature of the number 19 in the Quran, let us sail through one of the most commanding phrases in the Quran: *"Fattaqullaha wa Aṭi'ūn"* — "So fear God and obey me."

At first glance, it appears to be just a recurring instruction, but beneath its repetition lies a breathtaking mathematical symmetry, woven deeply into the structure of the Quran.

This phrase appears exactly ten times, distributed in three chapters: once in Chapter 3, then 8 times in Chapter 26, and finally once in Chapter 43. The specific verses are: **3:50**, **26:108**, **26:110**, **26:126**, **26:131**, **26:144**, **26:150**, **26:163**, **26:179**, and **43:63**. *Refer to Table 15.9*

VISIBLE SEQUENCE

43263	÷ 19
4363350	÷ 19
2612626179	÷ 19
2614426163	÷ 19
5821651361316116	÷ 19
(1478 - 53) = 1425	÷ 19

Fattaqullaha wa Ati'un

S.NO.	C		V	GAP	C+V	C-V
1st	3	:	50		**53**	47
#1	26	:	108	**58**	134	82
#2	26	:	110	2	136	84
#3	**26**	:	**126**	16	**152**	100
#4	26	:	131	5	157	105
#5	**26**	:	**144**	13	170	118
#6	26	:	150	6	176	124
#7	**26**	:	**163**	13	189	137
#8	**26**	:	**179**	16	205	153
Last	43	:	63	**116**	**106**	20
					1478	

Table 15.9

- All three chapter numbers (3, 26, and 43), arranged in reverse order (43, 26, 3), form **43263**, a number that divides cleanly by 19.

- Hidden beneath the first occurrence, the sum of all the chapter and verse numbers from the remaining nine appearances (134 + 136 + 152 + 157 + 170 + 176 + 189 + 205 + 106) equals 1425; no surprise, it is divisible by 19.
- The concept becomes more intricate. Within Chapter 26, the digits in serial numbers 3 & 8 as well as 5 & 7 combined are numbers in the multiple of 19 and form numbers that are multiples of 19. This means that the 3rd and 8th occurrences of the phrase *"Fattaqullaha wa Aṭiʿūn"* in Chapter 26, found in verses 26:126 and 26:179, when combined, form 2612626179, which divides perfectly by 19. Similarly, the 5th and 7th occurrences of the phrase *"Fattaqullaha wa Aṭiʿūn"*, located at 26:144 and 26:163, when combined, form 2614426163, which also results in a number that is perfectly divisible by 19.
- The remaining occurrences, 1st, 2nd, 4th, and 6th, when written together, form a 20-digit large number 26108261102613126150, divisible by 19.
- The last and first appearances: 43:63 and 3:50 written together as 4363350 is an exact multiple of 19.
- Applying all the occurrences with operators gives 2 results:

➔ (350 - 26108 + 26110 + 26126 + 26131 + 26144 + 26150 + 26163 - 26179 + 4363) equals **109250**, which is divisible by 19.

➔ (-350 + 26108 + 26110 - 26126 + 26131 + 26144 + 26150 - 26163 - 26179 - 4363) equals **47462**, which is divisible by 19.

- Can someone still argue that these examples are cherry-picked? If so, examine the sequence of gaps between the verse appearances - a structure no human could have subtly planted across dispersed chapters over time. Calculate the difference between each verse and its previous one: (108 - 50) = **58**, (110 - 108) = **2**, (126 - 110) = **16**, (131 - 126) = **5**, (144 - 131) = **13**, (150 - 144) = **6**, (163 - 150) = **13**, (179 - 163) = **16**, (63 - 179) = **116** *(absolute difference* *considered).* Now, string these gap values together, we get: **5821651361316116**. This 16-digit massive number, born purely out of the gaps between verse locations, is divisible by 19. Break it apart into 58216, 513, and 61316116; each segment is still divisible by 19.

This is not just mathematics; it is a fingerprint, a signature, beyond doubt, of the One who created both the language and the number.

* * *

Case #10- Al-Islam - *"Submission"* **(الإسلم)**

To consolidate our argument, let us examine the word *"Al-Islam"*. More than just a word, *Al-Islam* is the name of the religion that represents the pinnacle of religious evolution and serves as the foundation upon which our entire discussion stands. *Al-Islam* means peace, submission, and obedience. This profound term appears exactly four times in the Quran, specifically in Surah **3:19**, **3:85**, **5:3**, and **61:7**. Remarkably, the very first occurrence of *"Al-Islam"* is found in verse 19, a number that resonates with those who have walked the path of mathematics in the Quran. *Refer to Table 15.10*

Al-Islam				
	C		V	Append
#1	3	:	19	319
#2	3	:	85	385
#3	5	:	3	53
#4	61	:	7	617
TOTAL			114	1374

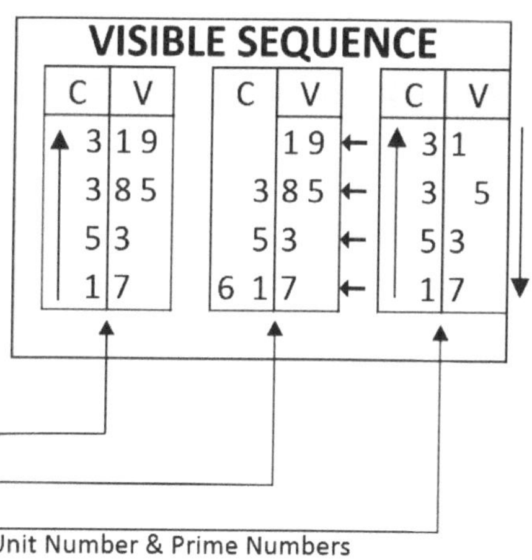

↑ 1533738159 ÷ **19**
← 7163558391 ÷ **19**
↑ 15331537 ÷ **19**
Σ **1374** <> 4731 ÷ **19**

Table 15.10

- The sum of the verses (19 + 85 + 3 + 7) is **114**, which is also the total number of chapters in the Quran and is a clear multiple of 19.
- Excluding the first digit (6) in the bottom row and combining the remaining digits, we find the sequence **1533738159** hidden in the columns. Testing it against 19 reveals that it is divisible by 19.
- Excluding the first digit (3) in the top row and writing the sequence in reverse order, we find **7163558391**, another tribute to 19.
- From the last two appearances, 5:3 and 61:7, the sum of the chapter and verse numbers (5 + 3 + 61 + 7) is **76**, which is divisible by 19.
- The sum of the appended chapter and verse numbers (319 + 385 + 53 + 617) is 1374, whose mirror number is **4731**, which is another clean multiple of 19.
- Finally, by listing only the prime numbers together with one (1) - the unitary number from both the chapters and verse numbers, the sequence formed is **15331537**, which is yet again divisible by 19.

* * *

Case #11 - A.L.M. - *"The Muqattaat Letters"* **(الم)**

One more striking example of the Quranic verse *"Over it are nineteen"* unfolds in Muqattaat, the mysterious letters A.L.M **(الم),** which appear at the beginning of six chapters: **2:1**, **3:1**, **29:1**, **30:1**, **31:1**, and **32:1**. *Refer to Table 15.11*

- If all the chapter and verse numbers are added (2 + 1 + 3 + 1 + 29 + 1 + 30 + 1 + 31 + 1 + 32 + 1), we get **133**, a perfect multiple of 19.
- Reorganizing the appended numbers into 2 sets of numbers and assigning math operators, we obtain: [(21 + 31 + 301) – (291 + 311 + 321)], which equals **570**, again divisible by 19.
- The sequence derived from the columns, **111112109323332**, is again a tribute to 19, as it is divisible by 19.

A. L .M. الم				
	C		V	Append
#1	2	:	1	21
#2	3	:	1	31
#3	29	:	1	291
#4	30	:	1	301
#5	31	:	1	311
#6	32	:	1	321
	127		**6**	**133**

+342 (#1 and #6), +342 (#2 and #5)

VISIBLE SEQUENCE		
C	C	V
	2	1
	3	1
2	9	1
3	0	1
3	1	1
3	2	1

1111112109322333 2 ÷ **19**

[(21 + 31 + 301) – (291 + 311 + 321)] = 570 ÷ **19**

(21 + 321) =**342** ÷ 19 (31 + 311) = **342** ÷ 19

[(29 - 1) + (30 - 1)] = **57** ÷ 19

Table 15.11

- The sum of the 1st and 6th occurrences (21 + 321) equals **342**, which is divisible by 19. Similarly, the sum of the 5th and 2nd occurrences (311 + 31) equals **342**, confirming divisibility by 19. Furthermore, the sum of the differences within the 4th and 3rd occurrences [(30 - 1) + (29 – 1)] totals **57**, which is also divisible by 19. Astonishingly, the number formed from the combination of the 1st and 6th, 5th and 2nd, 4th and 3rd occurrences, **165243**, is also divisible by 19.

This mathematical structure is not random, but rather deliberately designed, revealing the hidden presence of the number 19 throughout.

* * *

Case #12 - Kalimatullah - *The Words of God* (كَلِمَٰتُ ٱللَّهِ)

Among the many phrases scattered across the Quran lies *"Kalimatullah"* – the Words of God, a phrase that quietly conceals a remarkable numerical tapestry. It appears three times, at **6:34**, **10:64**, and **31:27**. At first glance, these references seem usual, yet when the numbers are woven together, the hidden code of 19 emerges once again.

Kalimatullah

	C		V
#1	6	:	34
#2	10	:	64
#3	31	:	27
	47		**125**

VISIBLE SEQUENCE

↓ 346427 ÷ 19
→ 1064 ÷ 19
→ 589 ÷ 19
<> 52174 ÷ 19

→ 3410643127 ÷ 19
↑ 7213460143 ÷ 19
↑ 31106263744 ÷ 19

(6 + 34 + 10 + 64) = 114 ÷ 19

(634 + 1064 + 31) = 1729 ÷ 19

Table 15.12

The chapter–verse pair 10:64 itself gives us the number **1064**, perfectly divisible by 19. *Refer to Table 15.12*

- Wherever the word *"Kalimatullah"* appears**, t**he sum of the Chapter numbers (47) and the Verse numbers (125) combined, results in 47125, whose reverse is **52174**, which is also divisible by 19.
- The pattern deepens. Exclude the first digit (6) and combine the remaining digits to reveal a hidden number **3410643127**, divisible by 19. Unbelievably, its mirror image, **7213460143**, shares the same property, being perfectly divisible by 19, which is rare.
- ***Special Note:*** *At times, the numerical structure seems to hold its secret just beneath the surface, as if one digit stands guard at the gate of revelation. When the first or last digit is excluded, the concealed order suddenly emerges, and the number aligns perfectly with the code of 19. It is as though the leading or trailing digit acts like a cap, a veil drawn over a hidden symmetry until it is lifted. Such occurrences suggest that the design is not arbitrary; rather, it hints at a deliberate structural alignment where even the positioning of digits carries meaning. Could this recurring phenomenon, where omission unveils precision, be a mere coincidence or an intentional marker left to test our perception of the unseen pattern?*

- In all the occurrences of the word *"Kalimatullah" there* are unused digits of the decimal system, they are 5, 8, and 9, which themselves unite to form a sequence **589**, yet another multiple of 19.
- When the verse numbers are appended, they form **346427**, another multiple of 19.
- From the first two occurrences, 6:34 and 10:64, the sum of all digits (6 + 34 + 10 + 64) equals **114**, a number perfectly divisible by 19.
- When all the numbers are written in sequence, column by column, the result is **31106263744**, a grand signature again divisible by 19.

What begins as a simple phrase – "the Words of God" – unfolds into a symphony of numbers, echoing the Quran's hidden structure. It is as though every occurrence, every omission, and every mirror image has been orchestrated to whisper the same truth - "*Over it are 19.*"

* * *

Case #13 - Munqaliboon - *Our Return* (مُنقَلِبونَ)

Examples are many, but our understanding is little. The word "**Munqaliboon**" (مُنقَلِبونَ), meaning *"Our Retrurn"* appears only three times in the Quran, at **7:125**, **26:50**, and **43:14**. *Refer to Table 15.13*

Munqaliboon					
	C		V	C+V	C-V
#1	7	:	125	132	118
#2	26	:	50	76	24
#3	43	:	14	57	29
Σ	76		189	265	171

→	7125 ÷ 19
↑	405251136724 ÷ 19

VISIBLE SEQUENCE

C	C	V	V	V
	7	1	2	5
2	6		5	0
4	3		1	4

Table 15.13

- The first occurrence is at 7:125, where **7125** itself is divisible by 19.
- The sum of the numbers of the second occurrence (26:50) equals **76**, divisible by 19.
- The sum of the numbers of the last occurrence (43:14) equals **57**, also divisible by 19. This final occurrence is in a verse composed of **19** letters: ﴿ وَإِنَّا إِلَىٰ رَبِّنَا لَمُنقَلِبُونَ ﴾
- The sum of the Chapter numbers (7 + 26 + 43) equals **76**, a perfect multiple of 19.
- The differences between Chapter and verse numbers are [(125 – 7) = 118, (50 – 26) = 24, (43 – 14) = 29]. The sum of the differences (118 + 24 + 29) equals **171**, divisible by 19.
- The sequence of numbers in columns is **4134056252**, which is divisible by 19.

These three coordinates of the scripture referring to the word "**Munqaliboon**" unfold an elegant mathematical pattern that feels more like intention and design rather than coincidence.

* * *

Case #14 - Haadha Siraat-um-Mustaqeem (هٰذا صِرٰطٌ مُستَقيمٌ)

Just to cast a final beam of light on the subject, consider the phrase *"Haadha Siraat-um-Mustaqeem"* (**هٰذا صِرٰطٌ مُستَقيمٌ**) meaning *"This is the Straight Path."* It appears only three times in the Quran, at **36:61**, **43:61**, and **43:64**. When these chapter and verse numbers are aligned column-wise, they form the sequence **344633666114**, which is perfectly divisible by 19. It is as if the *"Straight Path"* is not only a moral direction, but also a mathematically aligned way to 19.

Haadha Siraat - um - Mustakeem

	C		V
#1	36	:	61
#2	43	:	61
#3	43	:	64

* * *

Could all these cases be a coincidence repeated with precision? Or is it a structure constructed with perfection? These examples are but a handful of pearls drawn from an endless ocean. Though they do not seek to interpret the spiritual essence of "Nineteen", they demonstrate how its presence dismantles claims of human tampering. These examples show that despite the fog of historical uncertainty, the **mathematical architecture remains intact**. If history is a narrative susceptible to bias and alteration, then mathematics is the incorruptible record keeper.

Surrounded by 19

Examining one more overwhelming argument for the numerical marvel of 19 surrounding the Quran. The lens now widens to encompass not just words, not just individual letters, but the very framework of the Book from the Opening Chapters to the Heart and the End. *Refer to Table 15.13*

3 Chapters (Start)

	C		V	Append
#1	1	:	7	17
#2	2	:	286	-2286
#3	3	:	200	3200
				931

→ **931** ÷ 19
→ 7286200123 ÷ 19

Middle 3 Chapters

	C		V	Append
#1	56	:	96	5696
#2	57	:	29	5729
#3	58	:	22	5822
	171		147	17247

→ 569657295822 ÷ 19
<> 74271 ÷ 19
<> **74271741171** ÷ 19

Chapters (Last)

	C		V	Append
#1	112	:	4	1124
#2	113	:	5	1135
#3	114	:	6	1146
	339		15	

→ 456 ÷ 19
→ **33915** ÷ 19
→ 463524 ÷ 19

Table 15.13

At the beginning of the Quran, as a light of guidance are the first three chapters, whose verse counts are well known: **1:7**, **2:286**, and **3:200**.

- Stringing these together, first the verse numbers appended with their chapter numbers in sequence, we get the number **7286200123**. This formation is not random, but is a perfect multiple of 19.

- Take the appended chapters and verse numbers, add math operators to it to form an expression (17 – 2286 + 3200), the result of which is **931**, again silently but precisely divisible by 19.

Turning to the last three chapters of the Quran: **112:4**, **113:5**, and **114:6**. Their simplicity hides astonishing complexity.

- Appending just the verses 4, 5, and 6 gives us **456**, neatly falling into the arms of 19 by being divisible by 19.
- The sum of the chapter numbers is 339, and their verses total 15. Merge these two to form **33915**, and the seal manifests again, divisible by 19. The mathematics does not end here.
- And if all the numbers are written as a sequence, column-wise in reverse order, the resulting numbers **11146352411** and **11111434256** again exhibit the same rhythm, divisible by 19.

If the beginning and the end are marked with such pristine proofs of association with 19, what about the centre of the Quran? Do the middle chapters echo the same pattern? Of the 114 Chapters, the middle three chapters, along with their verses, are **56:96**, **57:29**, and **58:22**.

- When we string them, we get **569657295822**. The consistent pattern of 19 remains intact, as this number is also divisible by 19.
- Additionally, the sum of their appended chapter and verse numbers (5696 + 5729 + 5822) results in 17247, whose mirror number **74271** is exactly divisible by 19. The sum of the chapter numbers equals **171**, which is divisible by 19, and the sum of their verses equals 147, whose mirror **741** is also an exact multiple of 19. So, the entire mirror sequence 74271741171 is also divisible by 19.

Ended by 19

To put a final seal, perfumed with math if not scented with musk, we put forward the following argument:

- The phrase *"lil Muttaqeen"* (لِلْمُتَّقِين), which translates to *"for those who fear God," first* appears in 2:2 and last appears in 78:31 of the Quran. The difference between these appended numbers (7831 – 22) is **7809**, which is perfectly divisible by 19.
- In the Quran, 32 verses begin with the word Allah (**اللَّه**), spread across **19** chapters.
- The very first of these verses, which begins with the word *Allah*, appears at 2:15, while the last one is at 112:2; notably, the sum of the chapter numbers (2 +112) equals **114**. The sum (112 + 2) of the occurrence 112:2 itself also equals **114**, a multiple of 19.
- The center verse of these 32 verses, which begin with the word *Allah*, is the 16th verse, located at 30:40, where **3040** is divisible by 19.
- To conclude this pattern, the only verse in the Quran ending with the word "lillah" (لِلَّه) is **82:19**, where the verse number emphasizes the significance of the number 19.

"**Over it are Nineteen**" is not just a divine verse, but a divine Message. From **chapter and verse alignments** to **letter counts**, from **word repetitions** to **linguistic symmetries**, the patterns revolving around 19 demonstrate that human hands could not have orchestrated such a meticulous design. It binds the Quran's mathematical layout in a way that no editor, compiler, or historian could have arranged.

In this battlefield between history and mathematics, history appears like a weary opponent, rooted in time but limping in proof, while mathematics stands tall, revealing the structural skeleton of the Quran in digits and patterns. The Quran is not held together by parchment and ink, but by **perfect numerical stitching**, reinforced by the recurring presence of 19. The entire claim of incompleteness unravels in the number 19.

16

THE CLEAR AND EXPLICIT VICTORY

The battlefield lies quiet, the air thick with the weight of intellectual discourse. Mathematics stands tall, gleaming with the light of countless revelations, while History, though battered, remains a formidable presence. The echoes of their clash will reverberate through the minds of scholars, philosophers, and seekers of truth.

It is not merely about proving one's supremacy over the other, but about uncovering the truth that rests beneath the surface of the Quran.

History, noble and resolute, will acknowledge the weight of the evidence presented. The patterns, codes, and mathematical symphony within the verses all point to a design far beyond the capabilities of any human hand. The mathematical strikes and blows have not aimed to diminish the importance of historical context but to highlight the divine craftsmanship of the Quran.

Even if history remains vital, providing context, enriching understanding, and preserving the narrative of the past, it is through the lens of Mathematics that one can see the divine fingerprints and intricate design that prove the existing Quran is indeed a composition and compilation of God. Mathematics provides certainty where history raises doubt.

As the dust of the battlefield settles, History, though not vanquished, will have to acknowledge the supremacy of Mathematics in this arena. In the end, Mathematics will stand victorious, not by erasing History, but by illuminating a higher truth. History may have only a few narrations, but Mathematics knows no boundaries; it has countless examples to prove its point. The numerical wonders of the Quran are eloquent reminders of its precise compilation.

Mathematics has asserted that the Quran's compilation is not a product of chance or human intervention. The numerical patterns embedded within its verses affirm that its completeness and preservation are as undertaken in the Quran by God:

(Quran 15:9) *"Indeed it is We who have sent down the Message; and it is We who will guard it."*

(Quran 75:17) *"Surely it is for Us to compile it..."*

Consider a final example of verse (2:19), the 19th verse of Chapter 2, which is the first 19th numbered verse of the Holy Quran. It contains exactly 19 words, while the 19th line from the end of the Quran (111:2) also holds exactly 19 letters. The difference between the appended numbers of these verses (1112 - 219) results in **893**, which is perfectly divisible by the prime number 19. Such examples reflect the mathematical integrity of the Quran within its design.

The *Hija'i* alphabetical order, often dismissed as a mere human arrangement, now stands prominent as a divine sequence, meticulously proven through numerous examples. The once-debated order now gleams with clarity. In the battlefield of reason, History cannot deny the undeniable, and the truth that the Hija'i sequence is divine or was used by the divine is forever etched in time.

This battleground will continue to host new mathematical calculations within the Quran. Each discovery would serve as another strike against historical claims of alteration and human compilation. Mathematics has proven, beyond doubt, that History can be defeated in this arena.

The depth and complexity behind these patterns go far beyond what has been presented here. It is for the coming generations to continue this research with open hearts and curious minds, holding up the fact that the Quran is a miraculous book, compiled and preserved by God.

For more details and deeper insights into this fascinating subject, reach out to me at *faiyaz@hotmail.com*. The end of this journey marks a new beginning in the study of the history and mathematics of the Holy Quran.

History, though no longer the central figure, will gracefully accept this new understanding. The union of Mathematics and History would further the understanding of this divine text, for in the union of these disciplines lies the true path to knowledge. As the sun sets on this epic battleground, the conclusion is clear and undeniable. Mathematics has guided and helped in proving that God did not play dice with the Quran. The completeness and preservation of the Quran stand as a testament to the perfect knowledge and infinite wisdom of its Author, God, the Almighty.

He who has led you so far will guide you further – Rumi

FURTHER OBSERVATIONS

The observations presented in this addendum were identified after the completion of the main manuscript. These findings are included to encourage deeper reflection and to demonstrate that the mathematical patterns explored throughout this work continue to reveal themselves beyond the primary examples discussed.

Completeness of the Quran in Prime Numbers

Structure Of The Holy Quran - Prime Numbers							
Ch. Name	Chp #	Verses	Prime No.	Ch. Name	Chp #	Verses	Prime No.
Al-Fatiha	1	7	17	At-Takwir	81	29	109
Yunus	**10**	109	599	Al-Infitar	82	19	67
Ar-Ra'd	**13**	43	191	At-Tariq	86	17	59
Ash-Shu'ara	**26**	227	1433	Al-'Ala	87	19	67
Al-Ahzab	33	73	367	Ad-Dhuha	93	11	31
Ya Sin	**36**	83	431	Al-Alaq	96	19	67
Ash-Shura	**42**	53	241	Al-Qadr	97	5	11
Az-Zukhruf	**43**	89	461	Al-Adiyat	100	11	31
Ad-Dukhan	**44**	59	277	Al-Qaria	101	11	31
Al-Jathiya	**45**	37	157	Al-Asr	103	3	5
Al-Fath	48	29	109	Al-Fil	105	5	11
Al-Hadid	57	29	109	Al-Ma'un	107	7	17
Al-Mumtahina	60	13	41	Al-Kawthar	108	3	5
Al-Jumuah	62	11	31	An-Nasr	110	3	5
Al-Munafiqun	63	11	31	Al-Masadd	111	5	11
Al-Insan	76	31	127	Al-Falaq	113	5	11
			(32 CHAPTERS)		TOTAL	1076 +	5160
						6236	

Table F1-A

As one lingers over the numerical structure of the Quran, an understated yet eloquent pattern seems to emerge. Consider the total number of verses: 6236 - unchanged, unaltered, nothing added and nothing removed, exactly as revealed. Now observe a subtle path to this same total. If we focus only on chapters whose verse counts are prime numbers, and then pair each such chapter with the prime number that corresponds to its verse count - Chapter 1 with 7 verses leading to the 7th prime, 17; Chapter 10 with 109 verses leading to the 109th prime, 599, and so on—a remarkable convergence takes shape. When the verse numbers of these 32 chapters are summed, the result is 1076. When the associated prime numbers are summed, the result is 5160. *Refer to Table F1-A above.* Together, these two totals arrive precisely at **6236**. It is as though the Quran, through a different numerical language, quietly reaffirms its own completeness – counting and confirming itself.

A Repeated Opening of Glorification

As one reads the Quran attentively and repetitively, certain openings feel familiar, almost like echoes returning at measured intervals. Among these is the majestic declaration that begins with "*Sabbaha lillahi ma fee as-samawat...*"–a statement affirming that *all within the heavens glorifies God.* Remarkably, this exact opening appears at the start of three chapters: 57:1, 59:1, and 61:1. These chapters are not consecutive; they stand apart, separated by others, yet bound by a common beginning. When their chapter and verse numbers are written together – **571591611**, the resulting number aligns perfectly as a multiple of 19. A similar harmony emerges with a closely related opening, "*Yusabbihu lillahi ma fee as-samawat...*", which appears in two alternate chapters, 62:1 and 64:1. Once again, these chapters are not adjacent, yet when their numbers are combined as **626411**, the outcome is, once more, divisible by 19.

It is as if these openings point to a compilation marked by precision, where meaning and number move together, and where the multiplicity of 19 appears again as a subtle seal – silent, consistent, and unmistakably intentional.

Quran – the First Word to the Last

	Quran		
		C	V
First :	#1	10 :	15
Last :	#2	85 :	21
	Σ	95	

↑ 81502115 ÷ 19

The word **"Quran"**, distinct from *Al-Quran*, appears for the first time in Chapter 10, verse 15, and for the last time in Chapter 85, verse 21. These two occurrences stand like distant markers; when the chapter numbers of these two verses are added together, 10 and 85 equal 95, a multiple of 19. When the chapter and verse numbers are combined in sequence, it forms the number **81502115**, which is a multiple of 19, as if the opening and closing references are numerically tied across the span of revelation.

	بَلْ هُوَ قُرْآنٌ مَّجِيدٌ ۞ (85:21)											
	1	*2*	*3*	*4*	*5*	*6*	*7*	*8*	*9*	*10*	*11*	*12*
Letter	ب	ل	ه	و	ق	ر	آ	ن	م	ج	ي	د
In Surah 1	4	22	5	4	1	8	26	11	15	0	14	4
												Σ 114

Table F2-B

Another striking moment occurs in the final appearance at verse 85:21 – "بَلْ هُوَ قُرْآنٌ مَّجِيدٌ" – *"Indeed, this is a glorious Quran"*, comprising 12 letters. When each distinct letter of this verse is traced back to its frequency of occurrence in Chapter 1, *Surah Al-Fateha*, the resulting values – 4, 22, 5, 4, 1, 8, 26, 11, 15, 0, 14, and 4 – sum exactly to **114**. *Refer to Table F2-B above.* The number 114, which represents the total number of chapters in the Quran, is itself a multiple of 19. It is as if the Quran, in its closing affirmation, presents a numerical closure that points unmistakably to the totality of the Book – 114 chapters, complete and intact.

Qul – قُلْ ("Say") – *In the Beginning*

Qul قُلْ			
	C		V
#1	72	:	28
#2	109	:	6
#3	112	:	5
#4	113	:	4
#5	114	:	6
			49

72109112113114 ÷ 19	
↑	264568 ÷ 19

It is commonly taught that the Qur'an contains four chapters that begin with the word "Qul" (قُلْ "Say"). However, upon closer examination, there is a fifth chapter that is often overlooked: Surah Al-Jinn (Chapter 72), which also starts with the word "Qul." Therefore, the total count is not four, but five chapters: 72, 109, 112, 113, and 114. When the chapter numbers are placed side by side, they form the sequence **72109112113114**, which divides perfectly by 19, leaving no remainder. Additionally, the number of verses in these chapters follows a similar pattern: they have 28, 6, 4, 5, and 6 verses, respectively. When arranged in sequence (**265468**), this also aligns with the significant number 19.

This is not merely arithmetic designed to impress; rather, it reveals a coherent pattern for those who take a closer look. When the evidence accumulates without contradiction, belief is no longer something that has to be demanded; it arises naturally. In such instances, one is left not merely counting numbers but witnessing the miracle of God – The Holy Quran.

9 789357 596961

Printed at Repro India Ltd.